ZINFANDEL
COOKBOOK

Food to go with California's heritage wine

JAN NIX

MARGARET SMITH

TOYON HILL PRESS

WOODSIDE, CALIFORNIA

Copyright © 1994 - 2001 Janeth Johnson Nix & Margaret Acton Smith
Fifth Printing, 2001

Library of Congress Cataloging-in-Publication Data:

Nix, Janeth Johnson and Smith, Margaret Acton
Zinfandel Cookbook Food To Go With California's Heritage Wine
/ Janeth Johnson Nix and Margaret Acton Smith
    p. 112
    "Wine-friendly food series"
    Includes index.
    ISBN 0-9642901-0-3 : $17.95
1. Cookery. 2. Cookery (wine). 3. Wines.
I. Title.
                       94-60979
                       CIP

Book Editor: Barbara J. Braasch
Book Design, and Illustrations: Andrea Hendrick
Cover: Kathy Avanzino Barone
Cover Illustration: Rik Olson

Toyon Hill Press
118 Hillside Drive
Woodside, CA 94062-3521
www.toyonhillpress.com

Printed in Canada by Hignell Book Printing   Fifth printing

Contents

(Continued on next page)

Pasta, Pizza & Grains   61

Salads & Vegetables   77

Desserts & Drinks   93

All About Zin

The romance of wine begins in the vineyard and ends in the glass. Along the way, many traditions are developed. This is particularly true of Zinfandel, which holds a special place in the hearts and minds of many people.

A bottle of Zin may have introduced some to the joys of sipping wine, remind others of the fun of making wine, or simply evoke pleasurable memories of past family gatherings. And, as good wine goes with good food, a good Zinfandel will complement any meal.

All of the recipes in this book have been developed to pair with Zinfandel, America's Heritage Wine.

California's Zinfandel Growing Regions

Mendocino, Napa, Sonoma

Lodi

Sierra Foothills

Santa Clara & Santa Cruz

Paso Robles

A Peek Into The Past

They came by land and by sea, those early settlers of California. With them came grape vine and fruit tree cuttings, seeds, and whatever else was needed for survival. The grape vines were soon planted, yielding fruit that could quickly be made into table wine to accompany meals.

Along hillsides and in the valleys of what are now Mendocino, Sonoma, Napa, Contra Costa, Santa Clara, and Santa Cruz counties and the Livermore area, the pioneers planted a grape with special qualities. Making wine from it was uncomplicated; the resulting vintage was easy to drink when young; and, when aged, that vintage became a mellow, extraordinary wine. This coveted grape also flourished in inland areas as settlers moved away from the bay—to the Sierra Foothills, the Paso Robles region, and the "wilderness" of California's Central Valley. Along the way, the grape acquired the name of Zinfandel, though the origins of this name and of the grape's European ancestry remain a mystery.

How the grape received its name may be unknown, but the name is strictly American, and wine grapes by that name were grown only in California at the time. The state's sunny climate provided just the right conditions for Zinfandel. And, with no need for fancy trellising, Zinfandel was as hardy as the pioneers themselves.

After the 1849 California Gold Rush, timber and wire were scarce. But these wine grapes could be planted in a way that made harvesting possible with no special equipment. Called "head pruning," it's a technique still in use today. When you see a vineyard with vines standing about three feet tall without wires, you can assume that you're looking at Zinfandel. Many of these vineyards are still producing even though they may have passed the century mark. Some wine labels boast an "Old Vines" designation.

Much like the barn-raisings of the Midwest, the making of Zinfandel wine (affectionately termed "dago red" by Italians and others) was a community affair. Family stories from San Francisco tell of entire neighborhoods getting together at harvest time to make wine. The grapes would come by train from Mendocino, Napa, and Sonoma counties, and be loaded on boats for the trip across the bay to San Francisco. Cool basements in the city provided the perfect environment for fermenting the red grape, and helping hands were plentiful. And, once the wine was made, it was easy to transport from there to waiting tables around the area.

As early as 1876, the red wine from California was granted awards in blind tastings in Europe. Often Zinfandel was poured into decanters and served to much acclaim at estate dinners in America and abroad. Thus, this wine with no lineage quickly took its place with the best.

A Wine History

The story of the ups and downs of the wine industry reads like a soap opera. There were more producing wineries in California in the late 1800s than exist today. When the transcontinental railroad was completed in 1869, it became possible to ship wine across land to cities in the East, and the demand for California's wine increased. Then phylloxera, a devastating louse that eats the roots of grape plants, started nibbling and entire vineyards were destroyed. Grafting cuttings on resistant, native American rootstock eventually saved the industry in both the United States and Europe.

In 1906, the San Andreas Fault shook San Francisco, destroying not only wineries in the city, but also those in the surrounding countryside. And the drums of Prohibition began to sound. In January, 1919, the Eighteenth Amendment to the Constitution, known as the Volstead Act, was ratified. On January 20, 1920, Prohibition began in the United States. Wine was literally poured into street gutters under the watchful eye of the U.S. government. Fortunately, a clause enabling non-commercial production of a limited amount of wine was written into the law. Enterprising folk began making their own Zinfandel to drink at meals with family and friends.

The Twenty-first Constitutional Amendment repealing Prohibition was ratified in December, 1933. This bill gave States the right to make their own laws regarding transportation of wine into and within the state, a tradition that continues today.

Wineries had closed during Prohibition and vineyards had been planted to fruit trees. As the demand for red table wine outstripped production, Zinfandel was planted once again, and those vineyards that had not been destroyed were brought back to life. By 1940, more acreage in California was planted to Zinfandel than any other grape variety.

As the wine industry recovered, growers also planted new European varieties. While urban developers were busy replacing old buildings with skyscrapers, some vineyardists began tearing out old Zinfandel vines and replanting with European varieties that either yielded more tons per acre or had an impeccable lineage. But Zinfandel remained California's most widely planted grape until 1993, when it was surpassed by Cabernet Sauvignon.

Picking A Zin

Part of Zinfandel's appeal is that it's as diverse as its background. Though it comes in many styles, there are only three basic types: Red Table Wine, a Portlike Late Harvest, and White Zinfandel, a relative newcomer that is made like a white wine. Each has special properties.

All types start from the same black grape varietal called Zinfandel. Though production methods differ, a flavor thread of ripe grape, blackberry, raspberry, and black cherry is apparent. This fruity flavor and inherent sweetness makes Zinfandel popular with both sophisticated wine drinkers and those just learning about the pleasures of wine. These flavors also complement almost any food, from hamburgers to haute cuisine.

The flavor and alcohol content of wine are determined by the ripeness of the wine grape, which, incidentally, is much sweeter than a table grape. Depending on growing conditions, the winemaker decides when to harvest the grapes and what style of wine to make. All wine is made by adding yeasts to grape juice. The fermentation process converts the grape's natural sugar into alcohol and releases carbon dioxide into the air.

Zinfandel, Red Table Wine

Zinfandel grapes ripen unevenly within the bunch, creating a blend of flavors while still on the vine. Grapes are picked just at the peak of ripeness, with not too many individual grapes being over-ripe, or "raisins," and not too many under-ripe, or tart. The balance has to be correct to give the wine its complex flavor. Because sweet raisins release their sugar in the moisture of the grape juice, Zinfandel is one of the few table wine varieties where the sugar level can go up when fermentation begins. Zinfandel is fermented dry, meaning the yeasts have converted all the sugar into alcohol, leaving 13% to 14% alcohol in the wine.

Almost all grape juice is white. As a wine's color is derived from the skins, grapes for red wine are crushed and fermented with their skins left in the juice. These skins impart tannins, which help determine the wine's longevity. Like strong tea, tannins give a puckery sensation to the tongue. As a wine ages, these tannins diminish, and the wine becomes "smooth." Zinfandel has less tannin naturally than other red wine. As a well-made Zinfandel is aged, it loses its fruity character; varietal characteristics vanish; and the wine resembles other wines, such as older Cabernet Sauvignon. Vintage Zinfandel can challenge the best vintage Cabernet Sauvignon or Bordeaux wine from France.

In addition to varietal flavors, the taste of Zinfandel is also determined by the soil in which it is grown and the microclimate of its area. This is known as "regional character," and is a subplot for connoisseurs searching for the ultimate Zinfandel. Though all regions produce the distinctive fruit and berry flavors that define Zinfandel, an accomplished palate can discern regional differences by taste.

A fine red table wine, Zinfandel can be enjoyed with a meal soon after it is made. It should be served at room temperature. Opened bottles can be kept on a shelf out of sunlight for up to five days; some wines stay fresh even longer.

Late Harvest Zinfandel

Grapes for this wine are picked near the end of the harvest season. Many in the bunch have already dried, becoming raisins; flavors have intensified and high sugars have developed. The resulting wine is sweeter than regular Zinfandel and contains a higher alcohol content, usually above 15%. Unlike Port and Sherry, which have distilled spirits (usually brandy) added after fermentation to raise their alcohol content to above 18%, Late Harvest Zinfandel has nothing added. The Zinfandel grape's unique properties allow yeasts to live in this high-alcohol environment during fermentation until the alcohol level becomes so high that fermentation stops, leaving some sugar in the wine.

Late Harvest Zinfandel should be served at room temperature. Newly released wine and older vintages are both satisfying. Opened bottles stored in a dark area can keep for several months.

White Zinfandel

To make White Zinfandel, grapes are picked early when sugar levels are low and color is not too intense. Unlike the production methods associated with red wine, the skins are separated from the juice immediately after crush. Fermentation is stopped before all the sugar is converted into alcohol, leaving residual sugar in the wine and a 10% to 11% alcohol content.

White Zinfandel is known for its sweet, fruity flavor and its pretty color, which can range from pale pink to almost red. Like beer, it should be enjoyed soon after bottling. Seldom does this wine improve with age. White Zinfandel can accompany almost any food; it's particularly enjoyable as an aperitif.

Chill White Zinfandel in the refrigerator and serve cold. Leftover wine can be saved by pushing a cork stopper back in the bottle to keep out air and placing the bottle in the refrigerator. If placed on its side with the cork in contact with the wine, unopened White Zinfandel can be stored in the refrigerator up to a year.

Wine & Food

Wine and food share a certain mystique; they appeal to our senses, and we're curious to learn more about each of them. Even their sounds are fascinating—the "pop" of a cork, the "sizzle" in a pan. Going out for a good meal is like attending a theatrical performance; opening a good bottle of wine at home makes a casual meal sparkle. On those occasions when you have a memorable wine with a marvelous meal, the experiences live in your memory.

Over the years several myths have become associated with the pairing of wine and food: only certain foods could be paired with certain wines; and only knowledgeable people knew how to pair them. But, as Dorothy learned in the Wizard of Oz, you have only to look behind the curtain to find that there is no such thing as a wine "wizard."

As your palate becomes more discriminating through tasting, you'll discover how regional foods match the wines from the area, and how winemakers can influence the taste of wine. One famous winemaker has a slogan, "No wimpy wines." His bold, full, concentrated wine would stand up to highly seasoned dishes. However, most Zinfandels pair pleasantly with contemporary cuisine.

People intrigued with the details of matching wines to food will have a wonderful time tasting different styles of Zinfandel from wine regions around the state. Others, too busy to study these intricacies, may feel that it's enough to know that wine and food have a natural affiliation.

The recipes in this book have been developed especially to pair with Zinfandel. An adaptable companion for all food occasions, Zin can be an elegant vintage wine or a friendly family favorite. We include suggestions for both company meals and casual family fare. The wine's regional differences also make it a perfect foil for a sampling of California's diverse ethnic cuisines. Even those who don't share your passion for wine will enjoy these innovative creations.

All recipe ingredients can be found in supermarkets or specialty food stores. When wine is included as an ingredient in the recipe, it is clearly marked as to its style of production—Zinfandel (red table wine), Late Harvest Zinfandel, or White Zinfandel.

Enjoy!

Appetizers

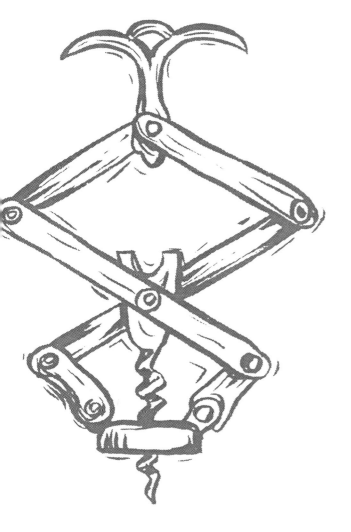

Handmade "concertina" corkscrew. 19th century

Hot and cold, light and hearty—we present more than a dozen fresh ideas for imaginative first courses and casual snacks. Whether you're entertaining many or only a few, this chapter will help get your party off to a good start. The varied suggestions range from a trio of easy-to-make toppings for crusty bread rounds to an eye-appealing cream puff wreath.

Also in these pages are the results of our tests to match cheese and Zinfandel. You may want to use our graph to plan your own tasting.

In this book, chile spelled with an "e" refers to fresh peppers and the product made from pure ground dried chiles. Chili spelled with an "i" can be a hot seasoning made from ground chiles and other ingredients or a stew such as Blue Ribbon Chili (page 37).

When handling fresh chiles like jalapeño or serrano, be careful not to touch your eyes. Wash any skin area that comes into contact with chile's volatile oils, most of which are concentrated in the interior vein.

Salsa Fresca

Sweet, juicy tomatoes enliven this fresh, summery topping for tortilla chips. If made a day ahead, add avocado just before serving.

> 1 pound tomatoes, coarsely chopped
> 1/4 cup chopped onion
> 2 tablespoons chopped cilantro
> 1 jalapeño, seeded and minced
> 2 teaspoons lemon juice
> 1 teaspoon olive oil
> 1 medium avocado
> Salt

In a bowl, combine tomatoes, onion, cilantro, jalapeño, lemon juice, and oil. Peel and pit avocado; cut into 1/2-inch pieces and add to salsa. Stir to blend; add salt to taste. Serve at once or cover and refrigerate up to 1 hour.

Makes 2 1/4 cups

Ten–Minute Salsa

When the vine-ripened variety is out of season, this quick salsa can be made from canned tomatoes. Unlike salsa fresca, which is freshly made, this salsa keeps for several days. Offer with tortilla chips.

> 2 cans (14 1/2 ounces each) diced
>   tomatoes, drained
> 1 can (4 ounces) diced green chiles
> 4 green onions and tops, chopped
> 2 teaspoons red wine vinegar
> 1/2 teaspoon dried oregano
> 1 teaspoon olive oil
> Salt

In a container with a tight-fitting lid, combine tomatoes, chiles, green onions, wine vinegar, oregano, and oil; stir to blend. Add salt to taste. Cover and refrigerate at least 1 hour for flavors to blend or up to 3 days.

Makes 3 cups

Creamy Spinach Dip

An oldie but goodie, this dip is perfect with the wide range of crunchy fresh vegetables.

$1/2$ cup *each* mayonnaise and plain yogurt
1   tablespoon lemon juice
$1/8$ teaspoon ground nutmeg
1   cup chopped cooked spinach, squeezed dry
$1/3$ cup chopped parsley
4   green onions and tops, chopped
$1/3$ cup chopped water chestnuts
Salt and cayenne to taste

Whisk together mayonnaise, yogurt, lemon juice, and nutmeg. Add spinach, parsley, green onions, and water chestnuts; mix well. Add salt and cayenne to taste. Cover and chill 2 hours for flavors to blend or up to 2 days.

Makes $2^1/4$ cups

Mushroom–Almond Pâté

A spread for crackers or baguette slices, this tasty topping is easy to prepare.

1   small onion, chopped
2   tablespoons butter
$1/2$ pound mushrooms, sliced
1   tablespoon dry sherry
$1/2$ teaspoon dried thyme
$1/8$ teaspoon *each* salt and pepper
$1/2$ cup slivered almonds, toasted
2   teaspoons almond oil or vegetable oil

Cook onion in butter until soft, about 5 minutes. Add mushrooms; cook for 2 minutes. Add sherry, thyme, salt, and pepper. Cook until mushrooms are tender and pan juices evaporate, 6 to 8 minutes. Place nuts in a food processor; whirl until very finely chopped. Add oil; process until nuts are pasty. Add mushroom mixture; process until mixture is smooth. Place in a small serving bowl. Cover and chill until ready to serve, up to 3 days.

Makes 1 $1/4$ cups

To toast almonds for recipes, spread them in a small baking pan and toast until golden in a 350° oven, about 8 minutes. Let cool.

Korean Chicken Wings

The caramelized marinade that glazes these wings, giving them a fruity taste, is a traditional Korean barbecue sauce. The chicken wings are luscious but messy and best served for casual affairs.

- 1 cup soy sauce
- $1/2$ cup Zinfandel
- $1/4$ cup sugar
- 1 large ripe pear (about 8 ounces), peeled, cored, and diced
- 2 green onions, white part only, sliced
- 2 large cloves garlic, crushed and peeled
- 3 quarter-size slices fresh ginger
- 2 tablespoons sesame seeds
- $1/4$ teaspoon black pepper
- 3 pounds chicken wings, separated into sections with tips discarded

In a blender, combine soy sauce, wine, sugar, pear, green onions, garlic, ginger, sesame seeds, and pepper. Whirl until seasonings are finely minced. Pour marinade into a pan and heat to simmering. Cook until sauce thickens slightly and is reduced by one-third. Let cool.

Place wings in a heavy, self-sealing, plastic bag. Pour marinade over wings; seal bag. Refrigerate 4 hours or overnight.

Preheat oven to 350°. Line 1 large or 2 smaller baking pans with foil. Pour wings and marinade into pan; spread wings to make a single layer. Bake, uncovered, for 30 minutes. Turn wings over; bake 15 or 20 more minutes or until wings are tender and glazed.

Serve warm or at room temperature.

Makes about 3 dozen

For best flavor, use only naturally fermented soy sauce; some brands are chemically hydrolyzed, which results in a harsh taste.

For another good dish, marinate Korean-style beef short ribs (ribs sawed across the bone to make tender strips of meat about 6 inches long and $1/4$-inch-thick) overnight in the marinade and grill quickly over hot coals.

Carnitas with Creamy Salsa Roja

Delicious with or without the dip, these "little meats" can be made with pork or turkey. If you use the leaner turkey, you'll need to add a bit of oil to facilitate browning. Serve carnitas in a heat-proof casserole and keep warm. Spike meat with wooden picks to dip.

2 pounds boneless pork butt or
   1 turkey thigh (about 2 pounds)
1⅓ cups water
⅔ cup Zinfandel
2 cloves garlic, minced
1 teaspoon ground mild red chile
½ teaspoon *each* ground cumin, dried oregano, and unsweetened cocoa powder
½ teaspoon *each* salt and pepper
2 bay leaves
1 tablespoon vegetable oil (optional)

Creamy Salsa Roja:
  1 cup sour cream
  1 cup bottled red salsa

Cut pork into 1-inch cubes, trimming fat as you cut. Or skin and bone turkey thigh, trim fat, and cut into 1-inch cubes. Place pork or turkey in a 5-quart pan with water, wine, garlic, ground chile, cumin, oregano, cocoa powder, salt, pepper, and bay leaves. (If using turkey, add oil.) Bring to a boil; reduce heat, cover and simmer 1¼ to 1½ hours or until meat is tender when pierced.

Discard bay leaves. Cook, uncovered, over medium heat until most of liquid evaporates and meat browns lightly, 10 to 12 minutes. If made ahead, don't reduce liquid until ready to reheat and serve.

Prepare dip: combine sour cream and salsa; spoon into a bowl. Serve with carnitas.

Makes 8 to 10 servings

Other uses for carnitas include wrapping the meat inside a corn tortilla to make a soft taco, tucking it into a flour tortilla for a burrito, or serving it as an entrée with refried beans and sautéed red and yellow bell peppers. For still more flavor, top with your favorite salsa.

Three–Way Toasts

Bite-size rounds of crusty bread topped with savory spreads and served hot from the oven are timesavers for a busy host or hostess. With toppings made ahead, the final assembly takes just a few minutes.

Baguette slices, cut ¼ to ⅜-inch thick, are our choice for the base. An 8-ounce loaf yields about 3 dozen slices. Top each slice with 1 tablespoon of the spread. Because the toppings are not soupy, you can spread slices a few hours ahead, cover, and refrigerate.

Bake toasts in a preheated 400° oven 6 to 8 minutes, just until hot and bubbly. Serve warm.

When you're only entertaining a small group, you may prefer to split the baguette lengthwise instead of cutting individual slices. To serve, put the bread on a board with a knife.

Chile–Cheese Topping

With its ever-popular blend of flavors, this Mexican-style taste treat is easy to fix and lasts for several days.

> 2 cups (8 ounces) shredded jack cheese
> 1 can (4 ounces) diced green chiles
> 1 can (4 ounces) chopped ripe olives
> 2 green onions and tops, thinly sliced
> ¼ cup mayonnaise

In a bowl, combine cheese, chiles, olives, and green onions. Add mayonnaise; mix well. Cover and chill up to 3 days. Spread on bread as directed above.

Makes 3 dozen toasts

Gingered Crab Topping

This bread spread is a perfect showcase for the sweet flavor of fresh Dungeness crab; canned crab is just too salty.

2 cups (12 ounces) flaked crab meat
$1/3$ cup mayonnaise
1 tablespoon Dijon mustard
1 tablespoon lemon juice
$1/4$ cup grated Parmesan cheese
1 tablespoon chopped cilantro
2 teaspoons minced ginger

Pick through crab and discard any bits of shell or cartilage. In a medium bowl, whisk together mayonnaise, mustard, lemon juice, and cheese. Stir in cilantro, ginger, and crab. Cover and chill until ready to use (no longer than the next day). Top bread as directed on facing page.

Makes 3 dozen toasts

Blue Cheese & Pecan Topping

A favorite French combination of flavors, this topping is also a grand match for Zinfandel.

6 ounces cream cheese, softened
3 ounces blue cheese, crumbled
1 tablespoon brandy
$1/2$ teaspoon dried thyme
Dash of cayenne
$1/4$ cup finely chopped pecans
Paprika

With an electric mixer, blend cream cheese, blue cheese, brandy, thyme, and cayenne until smooth. Stir in pecans. Cover and chill up to 3 days. Top bread as directed on facing page. Sprinkle covered toasts with paprika before baking.

Makes 3 dozen toasts

Panko is the name for dried Japanese-style bread crumbs. Coarser than crumbs made in the West, panko gives foods a crunchy coating. Look for panko in plastic bags in Asian markets, or make your own.

Trim crusts from firm white bread. Whirl in a food processor to make coarse crumbs. Bake in a 325° oven 15 minutes or until crisp and dry.

Chèvre Squares

With their great Greek flavors, these appetizers are party favorites. They require little or no fuss to prepare, and can be baked ahead and reheated at party time. The panko topping makes a crunchy contrast to the creamy filling.

1 cup small-curd cottage cheese
3 large eggs
1 clove garlic, cut into thirds
1/2 cup all-purpose flour
1/2 cup milk
1 cup (4 ounces) shredded jack cheese
4 ounces goat cheese (chèvre), crumbled
3 tablespoons melted butter
1/2 teaspoon dried thyme
1/2 cup panko (Japanese-style bread crumbs)

Preheat oven to 350°. Grease an 8-inch square pan.

In a food processor, combine cottage cheese, eggs, and garlic. Process until well blended. Add flour and milk; process until smooth. Add jack cheese, goat cheese, 2 tablespoons of butter, and thyme. Process until smooth.

Pour into pan. Toss panko with remaining 1 tablespoon of butter; sprinkle over the top.

Bake 30 to 35 minutes or until a knife inserted in the center comes out clean. Let cool on a rack at least 10 minutes. Cut into squares. Serve warm or at room temperature.

To reheat, place squares slightly apart on baking sheet. Bake in a 300° oven for 15 minutes.

Makes 3 dozen squares

Filo–wrapped Brie

When first cut, molten cheese oozes out of the flaky crust of this rich and creamy appetizer. We suggest spreading it on a sliced baguette loaf. Though the directions call for a cheese round, you can use a wedge. Simply split it in half lengthwise, place wedges together with ends pointing in opposite directions to form a rectangle, and wrap in four layers of filo.

    3 sun-dried tomatoes marinated in oil
       plus 1 tablespoon of the oil
    2 tablespoons butter
    4 sheets filo
    6 ounces round Brie cheese with rind

Drain oil from sun-dried tomatoes into a small pan; chop tomatoes. Heat butter with oil until it melts.

Trim filo to make 12-inch squares. Stack squares, brushing each lightly with butter-oil mixture as you stack. Spread tomatoes in center of stack in a circle about the size of the cheese round. Place cheese over tomatoes.

Fold one corner of filo over cheese and brush lightly with butter-oil. Fold over remaining corners, one by one, brushing with butter-oil after each fold. Press filo against cheese to make a smooth package.

Place wrapped cheese, seam side down, on an ungreased baking sheet. Brush the top with butter-oil. Cover and chill until ready to bake.

Preheat oven to 350°. Bake cheese, uncovered, for 20 minutes or until filo is golden brown. Let cool for 10 minutes before serving.

Makes 6 to 8 servings

Parchment-thin filo dries out quickly, so it's important to keep sheets protected from the air.

One way is to sandwich the stack of filo between clean dish towels, lifting off a single sheet as needed and covering the stack each time.

If a recipe doesn't call for an entire box of filo, place unused sheets in a sealable plastic bag and refrigerate. They will stay fresh up to 4 weeks.

Gougère

Traditionally served by French chefs with salad and red wine, this puffy cheese wreath also works well as an appetizer. Set the ring on a table and let people pull off their own puffs. Gougère tastes best when hot and crispy. You can bake it ahead and recrisp in a 300° oven, or make and shape the dough and chill up to 4 hours before baking.

1 cup water
5 tablespoons butter
1/4 teaspoon salt
Dash *each* white pepper and
   ground nutmeg
1 cup all-purpose flour
4 large eggs
1 cup (4 ounces) shredded sharp white
   Cheddar cheese

In a 3-quart pan over medium heat, bring water, butter, salt, pepper, and nutmeg to a boil. When butter melts, add flour all at once and cook, stirring with a wooden spoon, until mixture forms a ball, about 2 minutes. Remove pan from heat and beat in eggs, 1 at a time, until dough is smooth and well blended. Beat in 1/2 cup of cheese. (Or put dough in food processor and add eggs, 1 at a time, then add 1/2 cup cheese.)

Grease 2 baking sheets. Working with half of the dough at a time, mound 10 equal portions of dough in a circle so each ball of dough just touches the next one. Sprinkle 1/4 cup of cheese over the top. Repeat to make another wreath. If made ahead, cover with a tent of foil so foil does not touch dough; refrigerate for up to 4 hours.

Preheat oven to 375°. Bake puffs, uncovered, until golden brown and crisp, 45 to 50 minutes. If baked ahead, place puffs in a 300° oven for 10 minutes to heat through and recrisp. Serve hot.

Makes 10 servings

Sausage & Roasted Red Peppers

For a buffet, you can serve this savory hot hors d'oeuvre in an earthenware casserole with bamboo skewers. Or prepare it in individual parchment pouches to serve. Take your choice of specialty sausages, avoiding only a too-hot chorizo.

- 2 red bell peppers
- 1 pound full-cooked sausage, such as kielbasa, linguisa, or bratwurst, cut in diagonal slices ¼-inch-thick
- ¼ cup Zinfandel
- 2 cloves garlic, minced
- 2 tablespoons chopped parsley
- 10 pieces of cooking parchment cut into 10-inch squares (optional)

Roast peppers (see directions on right). Cut peppers into bite-size pieces.

In a wide frying pan over low heat, cook sausages until lightly browned, 4 to 6 minutes. (If using fresh sausage, cook for 10 minutes.) Discard pan drippings. Add wine and garlic; cook, stirring, over medium-high heat until pan juices evaporate. Remove pan from heat and stir in red peppers and parsley. Heat through and serve.

If wrapping in parchment, first let mixture cool. Dividing it evenly, place a spoonful in the center of each 10-inch parchment square; bring ends up to form a pouch and tie packet with a bow knot 2 inches from the top with raffia or string. Place packets in a shallow baking pan and refrigerate until ready to bake. Bake, uncovered, in a 350° oven for 15 minutes.

Makes 10 servings

To roast peppers, place in a shallow-rimmed pan, 2 inches below preheated broiler. Broil, turning frequently, until peppers are blistered and lightly charred.

Drop peppers into a plastic bag; seal. Let peppers sweat until cool enough to handle. Peel off skins, then discard stems, seeds, and veins.

WINNERS:

Dry Monterey jack
Blue cheese
Herb cheese
Parmesan

LOSERS:

Smoked cheeses
Sapsago

Cheese–Wine's Perfect Partner

Everyone has an opinion on pairing wine and cheese. Heated debates over which cheese goes best with which wine may outlast a party. In the end, of course, the choice of the right cheese for a wine variety is purely subjective.

There is agreement, however, that wine brings out the best in cheese and that cheese prepares the palate to enjoy wine. Whether served as an appetizer, as an ending for a meal, or as the traditional course after the salad and just before the dessert, cheese can enhance both the meal and the wine.

In the early days of this book, we invited neighbors and friends to a Zinfandel and cheese tasting. Though results were mixed, there were a few clear winners—and losers. If you want to plan a similar tasting for your friends, a copy of the grid we used is shown below.

Opinion: Two Styles of ZIN with Cheese

NAME OF CHEESE	YES	?	NO
Blue Cheese			
Brie			
Cheddar			
Dry Jack			
Feta			
Fontina			
Goat Cheese			
Gouda			
Gruyère			
Herb Cheese			
Jarlsburg			
Parmesan			
Sapsago			
Smoked Cheese			
Teleme			

Soups, Chowders & Chilis

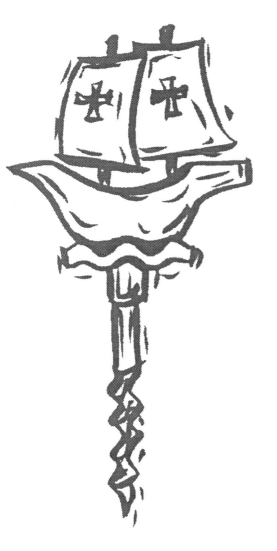

Brass ship corkscrew
Mid 20th century

For comfortable and casual fare, few dishes compare with soup. These steaming, fragrant, meals-in-a-bowl suit any occasion, and are sure to garner rave reviews from family and friends.

You need only the simplest accompaniments — green salad, good bread, fruit, and, of course, Zinfandel—for any of the innovative single-dish entrées. Though some of the recipe quantities may seem large, the idea is to make a lot to enjoy for several days.

Bell Pepper & Lentil Soup

Don't be tempted to substitute green bell peppers for the red ones in this colorful soup. The flavor of green bells would overpower the sweetness of the other ingredients, and crumple the best of Zins.

1 tablespoon vegetable oil
1 large onion, chopped
2 red bell peppers (about 1 pound), seeded and coarsely chopped
$1/4$ cup tomato paste
5 cups chicken broth
1 cup lentils, rinsed and drained
1 bay leaf
$1/2$ teaspoon *each* dried basil and thyme
$1/4$ teaspoon pepper
1 package (10 ounces) frozen baby lima beans
Salt
Chopped parsley for garnish

Heat oil in a 5-quart pan over medium heat. Add onion and bell peppers; cover and cook, stirring once or twice, for 5 to 10 minutes or until vegetables are soft but not brown.

Stir in tomato paste. Add broth, lentils, bay leaf, basil, thyme, and pepper. Bring to a boil; reduce heat, cover, and simmer for 30 minutes. Add lima beans and simmer 25 minutes or until lentils and beans are tender. Discard bay leaf.

In a food processor or blender, purée $1/3$ of the soup until smooth; stir purée into remaining soup. Season to taste with salt and heat to a simmer. To serve, ladle soup into bowls and garnish with parsley.

Makes 4 servings

The cooking technique called "sweating" is one we use to trim calories. In most of the recipes in this book, we sauté onions and other aromatic vegetables in a small amount of oil, covering the pan so that the vegetables "sweat" in their natural juices.

Cook vegetables over medium heat, stirring once or twice, for 5 minutes or until they are soft but not brown.

Curried Squash Soup

Just the right taste when the weather turns cool, this thick, flavorful soup is also perfect for packing in a thermos for football games or winter hikes.

- 1 tablespoon butter
- 1 medium onion, coarsely chopped
- 1½ teaspoons curry powder
- ¼ teaspoon *each* ground ginger and ground coriander
- 4 cups peeled, diced butternut squash (about 2 pounds)
- 1 large Golden Delicious apple, cored, peeled, and sliced
- 1 small carrot, thinly sliced
- 6 cups chicken broth
- 1 bay leaf

Salt and white pepper

Chopped hazelnuts or sliced almonds for garnish

Melt butter in a 5-quart pan over medium heat. Add onion; cover and cook, stirring once or twice, for 5 minutes or until onion is soft but not brown. Stir in curry powder, ginger, and coriander and cook 1 minute.

Add squash, apple, carrot, broth, and bay leaf. Bring to a boil; reduce heat, cover, and simmer 30 minutes or until vegetables are tender. Remove bay leaf. Pour off and reserve 1 cup of the cooking liquid.

In a food processor or blender, purée soup, a portion at a time, until smooth. Return soup to pan. Add reserved cooking liquid until soup is of desired consistency. Season to taste with salt and white pepper.

Heat to a simmer and serve in mugs or bowls. Garnish with hazelnuts or almonds as desired.

Makes 6 servings

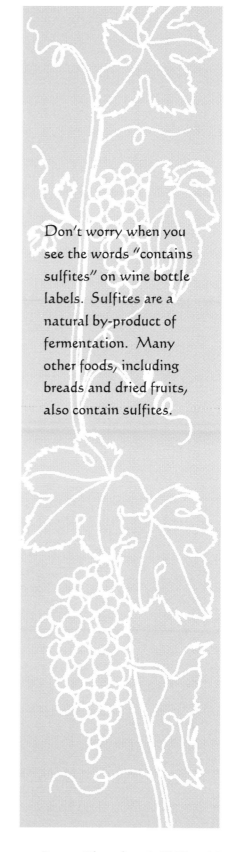

Don't worry when you see the words "contains sulfites" on wine bottle labels. Sulfites are a natural by-product of fermentation. Many other foods, including breads and dried fruits, also contain sulfites.

With its full berry flavors, a young Zinfandel pairs well with the mint and hot cayenne pepper flavors of this savory lentil soup.

Red Lentil Soup

Uncomplicated, satisfying, and as welcome the second or third day as the first, this soup is tasty, nourishing, and very easy to make. Except for their color, red lentils resemble the more common brown ones; look for them in markets that sell a variety of grains in bulk. Because rice makes a thicker soup than bulgur, use a little less.

 1 tablespoon butter
 1 large onion, finely chopped
 $^1/_4$ cup tomato paste
 4 cups *each* beef broth and water
 $^1/_3$ cup bulgur (cracked wheat)
  or $^1/_4$ cup long-grain white rice
 1 cup red lentils, rinsed and drained
 3 tablespoons chopped fresh mint
  leaves
Dash of cayenne
Salt

Melt butter in a 5-quart pan over medium heat. Add onion; cover and cook, stirring once or twice, for 5 minutes or until onion is soft but not brown.

Stir in tomato paste. Add broth, water, bulgur or rice, and lentils. (Red lentils stick together when wet; break up clumps with your fingers as you drop them into the pan.) Bring to a boil; reduce heat, cover, and simmer 40 to 45 minutes or until lentils are very soft. Stir occasionally as soup thickens to prevent sticking.

Stir in mint and cayenne. Season to taste with salt and simmer 3 minutes. Ladle soup into bowls.

Makes 6 servings

Onion Soup

Typically considered French bistro fare, onion soup's fame spread to this country about the time of California's gold rush. It became an instant hit in San Francisco restaurants, and is still popular. Though not traditional, Jarlsburg cheese is our choice for garnish; its buttery sweetness is a perfect match for the caramelized onions.

2 tablespoons butter
1 tablespoon olive oil
4 large mild onions, thinly sliced
1 tablespoon all-purpose flour
6 cups beef broth
$^1/_2$ cup Zinfandel
Salt and pepper
6 slices crusty French bread, toasted
1 cup (4 ounces) shredded Jarlsburg cheese

Melt butter with oil in a wide, deep frying pan over medium heat. Add onions and cook, stirring occasionally, until onions are soft and a rich caramel color, 30 to 40 minutes. Stir in flour and cook, stirring, for 1 minute. Add broth and wine and simmer 10 minutes. Season to taste with salt and pepper.

Ladle hot soup into oven-proof bowls. Float a piece of toasted bread in each bowl and sprinkle with cheese. Place in a 350° oven until cheese melts, about 10 minutes.

Makes 6 servings

A food processor makes short work of slicing large numbers of onions. If you use a chef's knife, cut the peeled onions in half lengthwise. Place the halves, cut side down, on a cutting board and thinly slice them crosswise.

Black Bean Soup

A good black bean soup is a standby, like a basic black dress or a gray suit. Sour cream-salsa topping adds eye appeal.

1 pound dried black beans
1 ham shank (about 1 pound)
2 medium onions, chopped
1 large carrot, chopped
1 stalk celery, chopped
3 cloves garlic, minced
5 cups *each* chicken broth and water
1 bay leaf
$^1/_2$ teaspoon *each* dried oregano and
   basil
$^1/_2$ cup Zinfandel
1 can (8 ounces) tomato sauce
Salt and pepper
$^1/_2$ cup sour cream mixed with
   2 tablespoons milk for garnish
Bottled salsa for garnish

Place beans in an 8-quart kettle with enough water to cover by 1 inch. Boil, uncovered, over high heat for 2 minutes. Cover and let stand 1 hour.

Drain beans. Add ham shank, onions, carrot, celery, garlic, broth, and water. Bring to a boil. With a large spoon, skim off foam that rises to the surface. Add bay leaf, oregano, and basil, Cover, reduce heat, and simmer 1$^1/_2$ hours. Add wine and tomato sauce. Simmer 1 more hour or until beans are very tender.

Remove shank with a slotted spoon; let cool. Cut off meat, discard skin and bone, and return meat to kettle. Discard bay leaf. In a food processor or blender, purée soup a portion at a time; return to kettle. Add salt and pepper to taste and heat to a simmer.

Ladle soup into bowls, drizzle sour cream-milk mixture over each serving, and top with a spoonful of salsa.

Makes 6 to 8 servings

Zinfandel wine is as good served in tumblers for casual meals as it is in crystal stemware for more elegant occasions.

However, Georg Riedel, head of the 237-year-old Austrian glassworks firm bearing his name, has produced a special crystal glass that he believes will enhance the properties of this unique wine.

The 14-ounce glass can be found at upscale wine merchants and department stores.

Mushroom & Barley Soup

A symphony of vegetables and herbs combined with barley, beef, and wine creates a stick-to-the-ribs, main-dish soup.

6 cups water
1 pound center-cut beef shank
1 can (14½ ounces) diced tomatoes, undrained
½ cup pearl barley
1 teaspoon dried basil
½ teaspoon *each* dried thyme and ground coriander
1 bay leaf
1 tablespoon vegetable oil
1 large onion, chopped
1 stalk celery, thinly sliced
1 clove garlic, minced
¼ pound mushrooms, thinly sliced
2 medium carrots, thinly sliced
½ eggplant, peeled and cut into ½-inch cubes
½ cup Zinfandel
½ teaspoon *each* salt and pepper
2 tablespoons chopped parsley

In a 5-quart pan, combine water, beef shank, tomatoes, barley, basil, thyme, coriander, and bay leaf. Bring to a boil; reduce heat, cover, and simmer 1¼ hours or until meat is tender. Remove shank with a slotted spoon; let cool. Cut meat into bite-size pieces, discard gristle and bone, and return meat to pan.

Heat oil in a wide frying pan over medium heat. Add onion and celery. Cover and cook, stirring once or twice, for 5 minutes or until vegetables are soft but not brown. Add garlic and mushrooms. Cook, uncovered, until mushrooms release their liquid. Stir vegetables into soup.

Add carrots, eggplant, wine, salt, and pepper. Bring to a boil; reduce heat, cover, and simmer 30 minutes or until vegetables are tender. Discard bay leaf. Add parsley and simmer 5 minutes. Ladle into bowls.

Makes 6 to 8 servings

Cooks use wine in a recipe to add liquid and flavor to broth. Wine's acids also help tenderize meats. The alcohol is evaporated during cooking.

Good cooks follow this adage: "Never cook with a wine you would not drink." That eliminates bottles labeled "cooking wine," which contain salt.

Meatball Minestrone

Using ground sirloin for meatballs may sound extravagant, but one pound is all you need for this crowd-pleasing soup.

Meatballs:
- 1 pound ground sirloin
- 1 large egg
- 1/4 cup fine dry bread crumbs
- 2 tablespoons Zinfandel
- 2 tablespoons chopped flat-leaf parsley
- 1/2 teaspoon salt
- 1/4 teaspoon pepper

- 1 tablespoon olive oil
- 1 medium onion, chopped
- 4 cups *each* beef broth and water
- 1 cup Zinfandel
- 1 can (14 1/2 ounces) diced tomatoes, undrained
- 1 can (about 1 pound) kidney beans, undrained
- 2 medium carrots, diced
- 2 zucchini, diced
- 1 teaspoon *each* dried basil and oregano
- 1 cup small pasta shells
- 1 1/2 cups sliced cabbage
- Salt and pepper
- Grated Parmesan cheese

To prepare meatballs, combine meat, egg, bread crumbs, wine, parsley, salt and pepper. Shape mixture into walnut-size balls.

Heat oil in an 8-quart kettle over medium heat. Add onion; cover, and cook, stirring once or twice, for 5 minutes, or until onion is soft but not brown. Add broth, water, wine, and tomatoes. Heat broth to a simmer. Add meatballs to broth and cook, uncovered, 5 minutes.

Add beans, carrots, zucchini, basil, and oregano. Cover and simmer 15 minutes. Stir in pasta shells and cabbage; cover and simmer 10 minutes, or until pasta is al dente. Season to taste with salt and pepper. Serve from a tureen or ladle into wide soup bowls. Pass grated cheese at the table.

Makes 8 servings

"I have many fond memories of growing up around red Zin.

Crushing time was a lot of fun for everyone--with group feasts at each other's homes. First tastings were another big event.

My father made wine in the old neighborhood (San Fancisco Bay Area) along with the other Italians.

My father and his neighbor had the best dago red Zinfandel in the country!"
—Quote from ZAP
  Zinfandel Express,
  May 1992

Tortilla Soup

Quick to fix and full of flavor, this popular soup offers south-of-the-border appeal. To cut down on preparation time, we suggest using leftover chicken and packaged tortilla chips.

Foods of the Americas and Zinfandel have a natural affinity.

The light tannins and apparent sweetness of the wine can cool the heat of chile in this recipe.

   2 teaspoons vegetable oil
$1/2$ cup chopped onion
$1/2$ cup thinly sliced celery
   2 cloves garlic, minced
   1 jalapeño or serrano chile, seeded and minced
   1 can ($14^1/2$ ounces) diced tomatoes, undrained
   4 cups chicken broth
   1 cup canned baby corn, each ear cut in half diagonally
   1 teaspoon ground cumin
   1 cup shredded cooked chicken
   1 tablespoon lime juice

Garnishes:
$1^1/2$ cups tortilla chips
$1/4$ cup coarsely chopped cilantro
$1/2$ cup shredded jack cheese
   1 small avocado, peeled, seeded, and diced

Heat oil in a 2-to 3-quart pan over medium heat. Add onion and celery; cover and cook, stirring once or twice, for 5 minutes. Add garlic and jalapeño or serrano chile. Cook 2 minutes or until vegetables are soft but not brown.

Add tomatoes, broth, baby corn, and cumin. Bring to a boil; reduce heat, cover, and simmer 10 minutes. Add chicken and lime juice and simmer 5 minutes.

Ladle soup into wide bowls. Garnish each serving or pass garnishes at the table.

Makes 4 servings

French cooks use a mortar and pestle (pistou) to make this basil sauce. We prefer the speed and ease of a food processor.

To prepare 6 servings of pistou, mince 2 large cloves of garlic. Process garlic, 1/3 cup packed fresh basil leaves, and 1/3 cup grated Parmesan cheese in a food processor until basil is finely chopped.

Add 1 tablespoon tomato paste and 1/3 cup olive oil, and whirl until blended.

Soup au Pistou

In Provence, home of this fragrant vegetable soup, a heady basil sauce (recipe at left) is passed at the table. Each person stirs in pistou to taste.

1 tablespoon olive oil
1 medium onion, chopped
8 cups water
1 can (14½ ounces) diced tomatoes, undrained
3 medium thin-skinned potatoes, peeled and cut into 1-inch pieces
2 medium carrots, diced
2 small leeks (tender white part only), coarsely chopped
1½ cups fresh green beans, cut into 1-inch lengths
2 medium zucchini, diced
1 can (15 ounces) white beans, undrained
1 teaspoon salt
½ teaspoon pepper
2 pinches crumbled saffron threads
½ cup spaghetti, broken into 2-inch pieces

Heat oil in an 8-quart kettle over medium heat. Add onion; cover and cook, stirring once or twice, for 5 minutes or until onion is soft but not brown. Add water, tomatoes, potatoes, carrots, and leeks. Bring to a boil; reduce heat, cover, and simmer 15 minutes. Add green beans, zucchini, and white beans. Cover and simmer 15 minutes. Add salt, pepper, saffron, and spaghetti. Cover and simmer 10 minutes or until spaghetti is al dente. Taste and correct seasoning.

Ladle soup into bowls. Pass pistou at the table so each person can add it to taste.

Makes 6 servings

Gino's Crab Cioppino

Though West Coast Italian fishermen take credit for creating this gutsy stew, the claim can't be substantiated. One of our favorite versions, which comes from veteran cook Gino Banducci in the Humboldt Bay area, is served over polenta. He starts with live crabs; you may prefer to buy them already cooked, cleaned, and cracked.

1/2 cup olive oil
1 large onion, chopped
2 large cloves garlic, minced
1 large carrot, finely diced
1 cup chopped celery
1/2 red bell pepper, seeded and chopped
2 cans (28 ounces *each*) crushed
 tomatoes with purée
3 bottles (8 ounces *each*) clam juice
2 cups Zinfandel
1 tablespoon *each* dried thyme and basil
2 teaspoons *each* dried oregano and salt
1 teaspoon pepper
1/2 cup chopped parsley
3 Dungeness crabs, cooked and cleaned
2 pounds ling cod or rock cod fillets
Polenta (recipe at right)
Garlic bread

Heat oil in an 8-quart pot over medium-high heat. Add onion, garlic, carrot, celery, and bell pepper; cook, stirring occasionally, until vegetables are soft but not brown, 12 to 15 minutes. Add tomatoes, clam juice, wine, thyme, basil, oregano, salt, and pepper. Bring to a boil; reduce heat, cover, and simmer 1 hour. Add parsley. If made ahead, cool, cover, and refrigerate until next day.

Cut crab bodies into quarters. Crack legs and claws so sauce will penetrate meat. Cut fish into bite-size pieces. If made ahead, reheat cioppino base to simmering. Add crab and simmer 20 minutes. Add fish and simmer 10 more minutes. Serve over polenta, and pass the garlic bread.

Makes 6 to 8 servings

Polenta

In a 3-quart pan, mix 2 cups cold water, 1 teaspoon salt, 1/8 teaspoon pepper, and 1 cup polenta or yellow cornmeal. Stir in 2 cups boiling water. Bring to a boil, stirring, over high heat.

Reduce heat to low. Cook, stirring, until polenta is thick and creamy, 10 to 12 minutes.

Stir in 2 tablespoons butter.

Makes 6 servings.

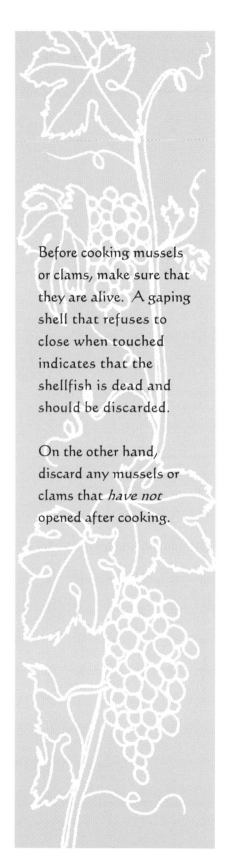

Before cooking mussels or clams, make sure that they are alive. A gaping shell that refuses to close when touched indicates that the shellfish is dead and should be discarded.

On the other hand, discard any mussels or clams that *have not* opened after cooking.

Holiday Cioppino

This dish is good for holiday entertaining because it's neat to eat. You can make the base a day or two ahead, but it's wise to buy seafood the day of the party.

1 tablespoon olive oil
1 medium onion, chopped
1/2 red bell pepper, seeded and chopped
4 cloves garlic, minced
1/3 cup chopped parsley
2 tablespoons tomato paste
1 can (28 ounces) diced tomatoes, undrained
1 bottle (8 ounces) clam juice
1 cup Zinfandel
1 teaspoon dried basil
1/2 teaspoon *each* dried thyme and dried marjoram
1/4 teaspoon *each* crushed red pepper, black pepper, and fennel seed
1 bay leaf
1 dozen mussels or small hard-shell clams
1/2 pound boneless firm white fish (red snapper, cod, shark, or halibut), cut into bite-size pieces
1/2 pound scallops
1/2 pound medium raw shrimp, shelled and deveined
1 jar (10 ounces) fresh oysters
Salt

Heat oil in a 5-quart pan over medium heat. Add onion and bell pepper; cover and cook, stirring once or twice, for 5 minutes or until vegetables are soft but not brown. Add garlic and parsley and cook 1 minute. Stir in tomato paste. Add tomatoes, clam juice, wine, basil, thyme, marjoram, crushed red pepper, black pepper, fennel seed, and bay leaf. Bring to a boil; reduce heat, cover, and simmer 30 minutes. Remove bay leaf. If made ahead, cool, cover, and refrigerate.

To complete, reheat cioppino sauce. Add mussels or clams and fish; cover and simmer 5 minutes. Add scallops and shrimp; simmer 4 minutes. Add oysters and their liquor and cook 2 more minutes. Season to taste with salt. Ladle into wide soup bowls.

Makes 4 to 6 servings

Tomato & Corn Chowder

Packed with vegetables, this easy-to-fix chowder is a family favorite. Simply top with grated cheese and serve with an herb bread from the bakery.

  1 tablespoon vegetable oil
  1 large onion, chopped
  2 medium carrots, thinly sliced
  1 stalk celery, thinly sliced
  1 can (14^1/$_2$ ounces) diced tomatoes, undrained
  2 cups thinly sliced cabbage
  3 cups chicken broth
  2^1/$_2$ cups water
  1 teaspoon dried basil
  ^{1}/$_2$ teaspoon dried oregano
  2 medium zucchini, thinly sliced
  1 cup frozen corn kernels
  1 cup corkscrew-shaped pasta
  2 tablespoons chopped parsley
Salt and pepper
Grated dry jack cheese

Heat oil in a 5-quart pan over medium heat. Add onion, carrots, and celery; cover and cook, stirring once or twice, for 5 minutes or until vegetables are soft but not brown.

Pour tomatoes into pan. Add cabbage, broth, water, basil, and oregano. Bring to a boil; reduce heat, cover, and simmer 30 minutes.

Increase heat until soup boils gently. Add zucchini, corn, and pasta. Cover and cook 10 minutes or until pasta is al dente. Stir in parsley and season to taste with salt and pepper. To serve, ladle soup into bowls. Pass grated cheese at the table.

Makes 6 servings

"Bread is made for laughter, and wine gladdens life, and money answers everything."
— The Bible
  (Ecclesiastes 10:19)

Thai Shrimp Chowder

A fruity young Zinfandel is the best complement for this aromatic fare. Though the chowder may look prosaic in the pan, when topped with fresh herbs it has a lively taste and a beautiful color.

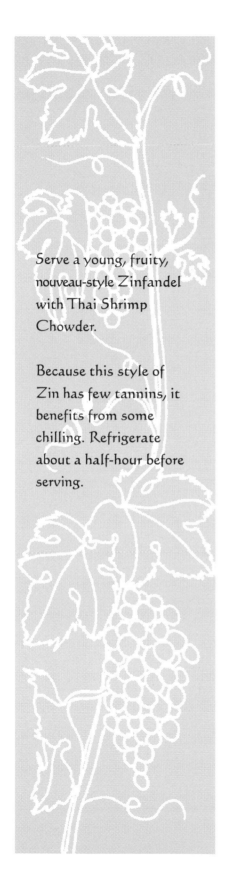

Serve a young, fruity, nouveau-style Zinfandel with Thai Shrimp Chowder.

Because this style of Zin has few tannins, it benefits from some chilling. Refrigerate about a half-hour before serving.

Spicy Broth:
- 8   cups chicken broth
- 3   quarter-size slices ginger
- 2   cloves garlic, crushed
- 2   stalks lemongrass, cut into thirds and lightly crushed
- 1   small dried red chile
- Shrimp shells, reserved (see below)

- $^3/_4$ pound thin-skinned potatoes
- $^3/_4$ pound sweet potatoes or yams
- 1   can (13$^1/_2$ ounces) unsweetened coconut milk
- 1   pound medium raw shrimp, shelled and deveined (reserve shells)
- $^1/_4$ cup *each* lightly packed cilantro, fresh mint, and fresh basil

Prepare spicy broth: In a 5-quart pan, combine broth, ginger, garlic, lemongrass, red chile, and shrimp shells. Bring to a boil; reduce heat, cover, and simmer 45 minutes. Strain broth and discard seasonings. Return broth to pan.

Peel potatoes and sweet potatoes; cut into 1-inch chunks and add to broth. Bring to a boil. Reduce heat, cover, and simmer until potatoes are tender, 18 to 20 minutes. Stir in coconut milk and shrimp. Simmer, without boiling, until soup is hot and shrimp turn pink.

Coarsely chop cilantro, mint, and basil; combine.

Ladle soup into bowls and sprinkle with fresh herbs.

Makes 6 servings

Blue Ribbon Chili

In official competition, it's against the rules for chili to contain beans, but we like to team tender bits of beef with plump pinto beans. If you prefer a sweeter flavor, try kidney beans or pink beans. On a scale of 1 to 10 (mild to searingly hot), this chili rates a 5.

1½ tablespoons vegetable oil
2 medium onions, chopped
3 cloves garlic, minced
2 pounds beef round, coarsely ground or cut into ¼-inch cubes
1 can (28 ounces) crushed tomatoes with purée
1 can (7¾ ounces) Mexican-style tomato sauce
2 cups water
1 cup Zinfandel
2 tablespoons mild ground red chile
1 teaspoon ground cumin
½ teaspoon dried oregano
6 cups drained cooked pinto beans
Salt
Chopped cilantro for garnish

Heat 1 tablespoon of oil in a wide frying pan over medium heat. Add onions; cover and cook, stirring once or twice, for 5 minutes. Add garlic and cook 1 more minute. Place onions in an 8-quart pot.

Heat the remaining ½ tablespoon oil in pan. Add meat; cook over high heat, stirring frequently, for 3 minutes. Pour meat and juices into pot. Add crushed tomatoes, tomato sauce, water, wine, ground chile, cumin, and oregano. Bring to a boil; reduce heat, cover, and simmer until meat is tender, about 1¼ hours.

Add beans; simmer 30 minutes or until chili is as thick as you like, stirring frequently to prevent sticking. Season to taste with salt. Ladle into bowls and sprinkle with cilantro.

Makes 6 to 8 servings

The bold flavor of a deep-colored, full-bodied, spicy Zinfandel would match well with the audacious flavor of the chili.

Unused tomato paste can be saved for another recipe.

Drop tablespoons of tomato paste on a pie pan, freeze until firm, place paste in a plastic freezer bag, and store until needed.

Chicken & Black Bean Chili

A mild flavor with a hint of spicy sweetness marks this chili. For an easy meal, serve it with flour tortillas and a Mexican-style salad of sliced oranges and sticks of crunchy jicama brushed with lime juice and sprinkled with salt and chili powder.

   2 cans (15 ounces *each*) black beans
   2 tablespoons tomato paste
   1 cup chicken broth
   1 tablespoon chili powder
   1/4 teaspoon *each* ground cinnamon, ground cumin, and dried oregano
   1 pound boneless, skinless chicken thighs
Salt and pepper
   2 teaspoons vegetable oil
   1 jalapeño, seeded and minced
   2 medium tomatoes, peeled, seeded, and chopped
Chopped cilantro for garnish

Drain liquid from 1 can of beans into a bowl. Add tomato paste, broth, chili powder, cinnamon, cumin, and oregano; whisk until blended. Drain the other can of beans and reserve liquid.

Cut chicken into 2-inch pieces; sprinkle lightly with salt and pepper. Heat oil in a wide frying pan over medium-high heat; add chicken and cook until lightly browned, 2 to 3 minutes on each side. Add jalapeño and cook for 1 minute.

Pour broth mixture over chicken; add tomatoes. Bring to a boil; reduce heat, cover, and simmer 20 minutes. Add beans and simmer for 15 more minutes. If you prefer a "soupier" chili, add some of the reserved bean broth and simmer for a few more minutes. Serve in deep bowls and sprinkle with cilantro.

Makes 4 servings

Meats,
Poultry &
Seafood

Silver-plated
corkscrew
20th century

As the recipes in this chapter illustrate, Zinfandel goes with a variety of entrées, from a delicious family-style beef stew to a salmon feast fit for tribal chiefs. It also pairs perfectly with many cuisines. Thai Chicken with Sweet Chili Sauce and Coq au Zin are only two examples.

Note also the offerings from three of our celebrity chefs. Their mouthwatering choices beautifully showcase the wine's adaptability.

There's something for everyone in these pages, including the host who likes to grill (Red-cooked Spareribs) and the cook who likes to make it simple (Five-Minute Shrimp).

Beef & Vegetable Stew

A silky gravy and vegetables cooked just until tender give old-fashioned stew a whole new look—and taste. To cut fat, trim the meat well and cook in a nonstick kettle.

- 1/4 cup all-purpose flour
- 1 teaspoon *each* salt and paprika
- 1/2 teaspoon pepper
- 2 pounds boneless beef chuck, cut into 1-inch cubes
- 1 tablespoon vegetable oil
- 3 cups canned beef broth
- 1 cup Zinfandel
- 2 bay leaves
- 1 teaspoon dried thyme
- 1 medium onion, coarsely chopped
- 4 carrots, cut crosswise into 1/4-inch rounds
- 6 medium (2-inch diameter) red, thin-skinned potatoes, peeled and cut into 1-inch cubes
- 2 tablespoons chopped parsley

Combine flour, salt, paprika, and pepper in a bowl. Dredge meat in flour on all sides; shake off excess. Heat oil in a 5-quart kettle over medium-high heat; add meat, a portion at a time, and cook until browned on all sides. As each portion is browned, lift out and set aside.

Return all meat to kettle. Add broth, wine, bay leaves, and thyme. Bring to a boil; reduce heat, cover, and simmer until meat is tender, 1 to 1 1/4 hours. Add onion and carrots; cover and simmer 10 minutes.

Add potatoes; cover and simmer until all vegetables are tender when pierced, 20 to 25 minutes. Discard bay leaves. Ladle stew into bowls and sprinkle with parsley.

Makes 8 servings

Drunken Steak with Shiitake Mushrooms

For dinner in a hurry, you can cook this range-top entrée in minutes. The deep, woodsy taste of shiitake mushrooms, the nutty aroma of sesame oil, and the pungent bite of ginger lend an Asian flavor.

10 dried shiitake mushrooms
2 tablespoons brandy
1 tablespoon soy sauce
2 tablespoons vegetable oil
1¹/₂ pounds New York strip, porterhouse, or other tender beefsteak, cut 1-inch thick
Salt and pepper
1 tablespoon minced shallot
2 teaspoons minced garlic
2 teaspoons minced ginger
1 teaspoon sesame oil

Soak mushrooms in warm water to cover for 30 minutes; drain, reserving ¹/₃-cup soaking liquid. Cut off and discard mushroom stems; thinly slice caps. Add brandy and soy sauce to reserved soaking liquid.

Heat vegetable oil in a wide frying pan over high heat. Place steak in pan and brown 2 minutes on each side. Turn heat to medium and continue cooking until meat is done to your liking, 3 minutes per side for medium rare. Season meat with salt and pepper to taste and remove to a warm place.

Add shallot, garlic, and ginger to pan and cook for 10 seconds. Add mushrooms and mushroom soaking mixture to pan; stir to scrape up browned bits. Cook until mushrooms are tender and sauce is reduced by half, 2 to 3 minutes. Stir in sesame oil.

Slice steak and arrange on a warm platter. Pour sauce over the top.

Makes 4 to 6 servings

California's cuisine reflects a melting pot of cultures. Zinfandel reflects a medley of styles – from nouveau, which is meant to be enjoyed while young, to a concentrated, intense wine that ages beautifully.

Cold Beef Tenderloin, Cajun–style

As Executive Chef for ARA Food Services, Louis Ferretti has cooked for presidents, prime ministers, and princes. His food is seductive, his presentation stylish. For regal entertaining at home, we like his spicy beef tenderloin.

Tomato Coulis

Sauté 1/2 cup minced onion and 1 clove minced garlic in 2 tablespoons olive oil 5 minutes.

Add 3 peeled, diced tomatoes; cook 2 minutes.

Remove from heat.

Add 1 tablespoon *each* balsamic vinegar, chopped fresh basil, and chopped parsley, and 1/4 teaspoon *each* salt and pepper.

Chill to blend flavors.

1 center-cut beef tenderloin (4 to 5 pounds)
1 tablespoon salt
1 tablespoon *each* black and white peppercorns and fennel seeds, coarsely crushed
1 teaspoon cayenne
1/4 teaspoon *each* dry mustard and ground nutmeg
1 large clove garlic, minced
1/3 cup melted butter
Tomato Coulis (recipe at left)

Horseradish Sauce:
1 cup mayonnaise
3 tablespoons grated fresh horseradish
1 1/2 teaspoons capers, coarsely chopped
1 1/2 teaspoons grated lemon peel
3/4 teaspoon Dijon mustard

Trim fat from meat. In a bowl, combine salt, black pepper, white pepper, fennel seeds, cayenne, mustard, nutmeg, and garlic. Add butter and mix well.

Preheat oven to 375°. Place meat on a rack in a shallow roasting pan. Rub spice mixture over all sides of meat. Roast, uncovered, for 50 minutes to 1 hour or until a meat thermometer inserted in center registers 120°. Remove from oven and let stand. Internal temperature will rise to 140°. When cool, cover and refrigerate up to 24 hours.

Prepare horseradish sauce: Combine mayonnaise, horseradish, capers, lemon peel, and mustard. Chill to blend flavors.

To serve, carve beef crosswise in thin slices and arrange on a platter. Serve with Horseradish Sauce and Tomato Coulis.

Makes 8 to 10 servings

Green Chile Pepper Beef

This recipe sounds hot, but it's not. It gets a peppery bite from black pepper and a subdued chile flavor from mild green chiles, but adding cream tames the heat. Serve with rice pilaf and sliced beefsteak tomatoes seasoned with balsamic vinegar and fresh basil.

2 green onions with tops, thinly sliced
1/4 cup canned diced green chiles
2 tablespoons chopped cilantro
1/2 cup canned beef broth
1 1/2 pounds lean ground beef or 4 small tender beefsteaks, cut 1-inch thick
2 teaspoons cracked black pepper
1/2 teaspoon salt
1/2 tablespoon *each* vegetable oil and butter
2 tablespoons brandy
1/2 cup whipping cream
Cilantro sprigs for garnish

In a blender, purée green onions, chiles, chopped cilantro, and broth; set aside.

If using ground beef, shape into 4 patties, each about 1-inch thick. Combine pepper and salt; press on both sides of meat. In a wide frying pan over medium-high heat, melt butter with oil. Add meat and cook until browned on both sides and done to your liking, 3 to 5 minutes per side for rare. Pour brandy around meat; cook until alcohol evaporates. Remove meat to a warm platter.

Add green onion purée to pan; cook, stirring, 2 minutes. Add cream. Boil over high heat until large shiny bubbles form and sauce thickens slightly, 2 to 3 minutes. Pour sauce over meat and garnish with cilantro sprigs.

Makes 4 servings

To match wines and food, think about their flavors. If some of the food flavors are present in the wine, it's a perfect marriage.

A Zinfandel described as having spicy black pepper flavor intertwined with its fruit flavors would pair perfectly with this beef dish.

Picnics, potlucks, and pigskin parties — Zinfandel is a friendly wine that can be enjoyed at every festive occasion. Its versatility makes it a good choice for almost any dish, from beef sandwiches to cioppino.

Party Beef Sandwiches

When sports fans gather at your house for the Big Game, a make-ahead beef brisket is your ticket to front-row viewing. Serve sandwich mixings as a fix-your-own buffet with onions, peppers, and German Potato Salad (page 79).

    1 beef brisket (3 to 4 pounds)
    2 teaspoons vegetable oil
    1 large onion, chopped
    2 cloves garlic, minced
    ½ cup Zinfandel
    2 tablespoons Worcestershire sauce
    1 tablespoon coarse-grain mustard
    ¼ teaspoon *each* salt and pepper
    Caramelized Onions (page 86)
    Roasted Red Peppers (page 21)
    Coarse-grain mustard
    Rye bread

Trim fat from meat. Place meat in a 9 by 13-inch glass baking dish. Heat oil in a wide frying pan over medium-low heat. Add onion, cover, and cook 5 minutes. Stir in garlic, wine, Worcestershire, mustard, salt, and pepper; simmer, uncovered, 1 minute. Pour over meat; turn meat to coat both sides. Cover dish tightly with foil. Bake in a 300° oven until meat is very tender when pierced, 3½ to 4 hours.

Remove meat from oven, let stand 10 minutes, then slice across the grain and arrange on serving platter. Skim fat from pan juices; drizzle a few spoonfuls of sauce over meat. Serve warm or at room temperature.

If made ahead, cool, cover, and chill up to 2 days. Slice meat, cover with jellied meat juices, and reheat in a microwave oven, or cover and heat in 350° oven 30 minutes.

For sandwiches, offer brisket, onions, peppers, mustard, and bread, and let guests make their own.

Makes 10 to 12 servings

Greek Meat Loaf

This meat loaf is a chameleon: it looks alarmingly messy as it bakes in the pan, but becomes an elegant entrée when served on a platter. To serve warm, cut the loaf in thick slices; for picnic fare or workaday sandwiches, slice thinner.

2   pounds lean ground beef
2   slices French bread, crusts removed, soaked in hot water, squeezed dry
1   medium onion, finely chopped
2   cloves garlic, minced
1   large egg
1/2   cup Zinfandel
1/2   teaspoon *each* salt and dried oregano
1/4   teaspoon pepper

Filling:
1   package (10 ounces) frozen chopped spinach, thawed and squeezed dry
2   tablespoons chopped flat-leaf parsley
2   large eggs
6   ounces feta cheese, crumbled

Topping:
1/3   cup catsup
3/4   teaspoon ground cinnamon

Place meat, bread, onion, garlic, egg, wine, salt, oregano, and pepper in a large bowl; mix well. On a sheet of foil, pat meat mixture into a 10 by 12-inch rectangle.

In a bowl, combine filling ingredients. Spread over meat, leaving a 1-inch margin on all sides. Using foil to help you lift, start with a 12-inch side and roll up jelly-roll style; press to seal all edges.

Place roll in a 9 by 13-inch baking pan. Bake in 375° oven 1 hour. Whisk catsup and cinnamon until smooth; brush on all sides of roll. Return to oven and bake 15 more minutes. Remove meat from oven and let stand 10 minutes. Using two spatulas, transfer meat to serving plate.

Makes 8 servings

When you decant an older wine to get rid of sediment, gently shake the bottle then let it stand quietly upright for 2 days. This procedure allows the loose sediment to drift to the bottom of the bottle.

When ready to decant, carefully tilt the bottle and slowly pour the wine into a decanter. Stop pouring when the sediment rises to the lip of the bottle.

If you don't have time to decant properly, pouring wine through a coffee filter removes most of the sediment.

To remove red wine stains from napkins, don't use water immediately. Soak the stain with white wine first, and then pour hot water through the cloth.

Herb–roasted Lamb

Just as lamb's flavor is enhanced by a glass of Zinfandel, its savory richness is heightened by garlic, sage, rosemary, and thyme. Terrific on a leg of lamb, this herbal infusion also works well as a marinade and basting sauce for lamb shish kebabs.

1 boned and rolled leg of lamb
   (3 to 4 pounds)
1 cup Zinfandel
¼ cup olive oil
4 cloves garlic, minced
1½ tablespoons fresh or 1½ teaspoons
   dried thyme
1 tablespoon *each* fresh or 1 teaspoon
   each dried rosemary and sage
2 bay leaves, crumbled
1 teaspoon salt
½ teaspoon pepper

Place lamb in a heavy self-sealing plastic bag. Combine wine, oil, garlic, thyme, rosemary, sage, bay leaves, salt, and pepper. Pour over meat; seal bag. Refrigerate 4 to 6 hours or overnight.

Remove meat from marinade and place on a rack in a shallow roasting pan. Strain herbs from marinade, reserving liquid. In a blender, purée herbs with 2 tablespoons of reserved marinade. Spread purée on all sides of meat.

Preheat oven to 325°. Roast meat, uncovered, until meat thermometer registers 140° for rare, 25 to 30 minutes per pound. Let rest 15 minutes before carving. Skim fat from pan drippings; reheat drippings and pass at the table.

Makes 8 to 10 servings

Moroccan Lamb Shanks

The sweetness of fruit acts as a counterpoint to the richness of these lamb shanks. Couscous or rice and chutney make fine accompaniments. To serve in a more elegant manner—or to stretch four shanks for six people, cut the meat off the bones before placing in a serving bowl.

- 4 lamb shanks
- 1 tablespoon vegetable oil
- 1 medium onion, chopped
- 1 clove garlic, minced
- 1 teaspoon ground ginger
- $^1/_2$ teaspoon ground cumin
- $^1/_4$ teaspoon *each* salt and pepper
- Pinch of cayenne
- 4 *each* dried pears and dried peaches, cut in half
- 8 pitted prunes
- $^3/_4$ cup Zinfandel
- $2^1/_2$ cups chicken broth
- 2 tablespoons chopped cilantro

Trim fat from shanks. Heat oil in a 5-quart pan over medium-high heat. Add shanks and cook until lightly browned on all sides, about 15 minutes. Lift out and set aside. Reduce heat to medium. Add onion and garlic and cook 3 minutes. Stir in ginger, cumin, salt, pepper, and cayenne. Return shanks to pan; add pears, peaches, prunes, wine, and 2 cups of the broth.

Bring to a boil; cover, reduce heat, and simmer until meat pulls easily from bone, 2 to $2^1/_2$ hours. Turn shanks every 30 minutes and add more broth as needed until shanks are halfway covered.

Lift out shanks and fruit and place in a serving bowl. Skim fat from pan juices. Reduce pan juices over medium heat until slightly thickened and syrupy. Pour over meat and sprinkle with cilantro.

Makes 4 to 6 servings

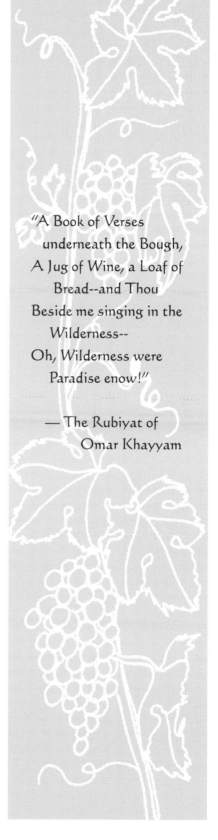

"A Book of Verses
    underneath the Bough,
A Jug of Wine, a Loaf of
    Bread--and Thou
Beside me singing in the
    Wilderness--
Oh, Wilderness were
    Paradise enow!"

— The Rubiyat of
    Omar Khayyam

Red–cooked Spareribs

Red-cooking, an age-old Chinese technique, gets its name from the mahogany color meats gain when simmered in a highly seasoned soy sauce. You can use the cooking liquid, called "master sauce," again and again. The more you use it, the richer and rounder its flavor becomes. We reduced part of the sauce and thickened it slightly to use as a barbecue basting glaze.

- 4 pounds pork spareribs or baby back ribs
- 8 cups water
- $2/3$ cup dry sherry
- $1/2$ cup regular soy sauce
- $1/2$ cup dark soy sauce
- $1/3$ cup sugar
- $1/4$ cup sliced ginger, crushed
- 8 cloves garlic, crushed
- 1 teaspoon Szechwan peppercorns
- 2 star anise
- 2 tablespoons cornstarch
- 3 tablespoons water

Cut ribs into serving-size pieces; trim fat. In a deep pot, simmer 8 cups water, sherry, soy sauces, sugar, ginger, garlic, Szechwan peppercorns, and star anise, covered, 20 minutes. Place ribs in pot and simmer, covered, 50 minutes.

Lift out ribs and set aside. Strain sauce. Return 4 cups sauce to pot for making basting glaze; save remaining sauce to use another time, if desired. Cook sauce, uncovered, over medium heat until reduced by half (2 cups), 10 to 15 minutes. Blend cornstarch and 3 tablespoons water; add to pot and cook, stirring until thickened, about 1 minute.

Preheat charcoal grill and grease rack. Place ribs 4 to 6 inches above coals and cook until lightly browned, 10 to 15 minutes. Brush thickened sauce over all sides. Grill, brushing frequently with sauce, until ribs are tender and well glazed, 5 to 7 minutes per side.

Makes 6 to 8 servings

Not related to black peppercorns, Szechwan peppercorns are reddish-brown dried berries that leave the mouth with a pleasant numbing feeling rather than a hot, burning sensation.

A licorice-flavored star anise pod contains eight points, but most pods come broken; just figure eight broken points equals one pod.

Look for both ingredients in Asian markets. A small package of either one yields enough for dozens of Chinese dishes.

Roast Chicken with Honey–Hoisin Glaze

Our good friend Martin Yan, star of the PBS series "Yan Can Cook," suggests roast chicken as the perfect partner to Zin. This choice, from his book Everybody's Wokking (Harlow & Ratner, 1991), is easy to prepare—and incredibly delicious. Roasting two chickens at a time leaves leftovers for sandwiches or Chinese Chicken Salad (page 81).

1 whole frying chicken (3 to 3¹/₂ pounds)
1 tablespoon soy sauce
¹/₂ teaspoon salt
¹/₂ teaspoon Chinese five-spice
2 thin slices ginger, crushed
2 cloves garlic, crushed

Honey-Hoisin Glaze:
1¹/₂ tablespoons soy sauce
1 tablespoon hoisin sauce
2 teaspoons honey
1 teaspoon sesame oil

Run your fingers between the skin and flesh over chicken breast and legs. In a small bowl, combine soy sauce, salt, and Chinese five-spice. Rub half of mixture on flesh under skin. Rub remaining mixture on top of skin. Place crushed ginger and garlic under skin on breast. Wrap chicken in plastic and refrigerate for at least 2 hours or overnight.

Preheat oven to 375°. Place chicken, breast down, on rack in shallow baking pan. Bake, uncovered, for 30 minutes. Turn chicken over and bake 30 more minutes. Brush with glaze; bake until meat at thighbone is no longer pink when cut, 10 to 15 minutes.

Makes 4 to 6 servings

"When one glass of wine invites the second, the wine is good."
— Samuele Sebastiani

Peeling onions takes time, but you can speed up the process, and avoid tears, by blanching them first.

Drop unpeeled onions in a pan of boiling water, turn off the heat, and let onions stand 3 minutes; drain.

When cool, trim root and stem ends and slip off the skins.

Coq au Zin

The French call this delicious braised chicken dish coq au vin. *We call it "coq au Zin" because the name and flavor change with the wine used for its cooking, and Zinfandel's berry flavor is evident in this recipe.*

4   chicken legs and thighs, cut apart
Salt and pepper
1/4 pound lean ham, cut into 1/4-inch cubes
1   tablespoon vegetable oil
8   small onions, 1 to 1 1/2 inch diameter
1/2 pound small mushrooms
1   clove garlic, minced
1 1/2 cups canned beef broth
2   tablespoons Dijon mustard
1   cup Zinfandel
1/4 teaspoon dried thyme leaves
1   bay leaf
1   tablespoon *each* cornstarch and water
2   tablespoons chopped parsley

Sprinkle chicken with salt and pepper. In a wide frying pan over medium-high heat, cook ham in 1 teaspoon of oil until lightly browned; remove from pan. Add 1 more teaspoon of oil to pan and cook chicken until golden brown. Add to ham. Add the remaining teaspoon of oil and onions to pan; cook until lightly browned, 6 to 8 minutes. Add to chicken and ham.

Add mushrooms, garlic, and 2 tablespoons of broth to pan. Cook, uncovered, until liquid has evaporated and mushrooms are golden brown. Return chicken, onions, and ham to pan. Combine mustard, the remaining broth, wine, and thyme. Pour over chicken. Add bay leaf.

Bring to a boil; reduce heat, cover, and simmer until meat near bone is no longer pink when cut, 35 to 40 minutes. Discard bay leaf. Place chicken and vegetables in a serving bowl. Over high heat, reduce pan juices to 1 1/2 cups. Mix cornstarch and water; stir into juices. Cook, stirring, until sauce boils. Pour over chicken and sprinkle with parsley.

Makes 4 servings

Chicken & Sweet Peppers

Close your eyes when you take your first taste of this classic Spanish dish and you'll feel like you're dining on the Costa del Sol. The Mediterranean flavors of olive oil and sweet peppers and the butttery accent of olives adapt equally well to California cuisine.

    1 frying chicken (3 to 4 pounds), cut up
    Salt and pepper
    1 tablespoon olive oil
    2 medium onions, sliced lengthwise
    1 *each* red and yellow bell pepper, seeded and thinly sliced
    1 clove garlic, minced
    2 ounces prosciutto, minced
    1 can (14$^{1}/_{2}$ ounces) cut tomatoes, undrained
    8 *each* green Spanish olives and black olives
    2 tablespoons chopped parsley

Sprinkle chicken with salt and pepper. Heat oil in a wide frying pan over medium-high heat. Add chicken and cook until lightly browned, 4 to 5 minutes per side. Lift out and set aside.

Add onions, bell peppers, garlic, and prosciutto to pan. Cook over medium heat, stirring frequently, until vegetables are soft but not brown. Add tomatoes and olives.

Return chicken to pan. Bring to a boil; reduce heat, cover, and simmer until meat near bone is no longer pink when cut, 35 to 40 minutes. Lift out chicken and place in serving bowl. Simmer sauce over medium heat until it thickens slightly and juices are syrupy. Pour sauce over chicken and sprinkle with parsley.

Makes 4 to 6 servings

In many families, it has become a tradition to serve wine at special family meals.

The wine gives people an opportunity to slow down and savor both the food and the conversation.

Chicken Caponata

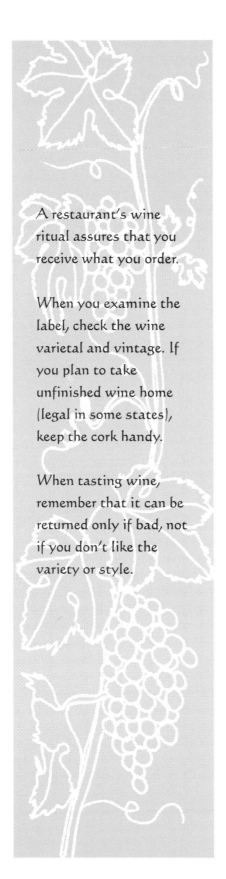

Located in St. Helena, the heart of California's Wine Country, Showley's at Miramonte is a favorite dining destination for local winemakers and tourists alike. Their menus complement both area wines and vintages from around the world. Zinfandel, a staff favorite, is always on the wine list.

1/2 medium eggplant, unpeeled and cut into 3/4-inch cubes
3 tablespoons olive oil
3/4 cup *each* coarsely chopped onion and celery
1 cup *each* diced zucchini, peeled Italian tomatoes, and red bell pepper
2 cloves garlic, minced
1 teaspoon anchovy paste
2 teaspoons capers
1/2 teaspoon dried oregano
6 boneless, skinless chicken breast halves
Salt and pepper
1/2 cup Zinfandel

Sprinkle eggplant with salt and let drain in a colander 30 minutes. Rinse and pat dry with paper towels. Heat 1 tablespoon of oil in a wide frying pan over medium-high heat. Add eggplant and cook until golden, 4 to 5 minutes.

Add 1 more tablespoon of oil, onion, and celery to pan. Cook 5 minutes. Add zucchini, tomatoes, bell pepper, garlic, anchovy paste, capers, and oregano. Cover and cook, stirring occasionally, over low heat for 15 minutes.

Sprinkle chicken with salt and pepper. Heat remaining 1 tablespoon oil in a wide frying pan over medium-high heat. Add chicken and cook until lightly browned, 3 minutes per side. Pour caponata over chicken. Add wine. Bring to a boil; reduce heat, cover, and simmer until vegetables are tender and chicken is no longer pink when cut, 10 to 15 minutes. Add salt and pepper to taste.

Makes 6 servings

A restaurant's wine ritual assures that you receive what you order.

When you examine the label, check the wine varietal and vintage. If you plan to take unfinished wine home (legal in some states), keep the cork handy.

When tasting wine, remember that it can be returned only if bad, not if you don't like the variety or style.

Thai Chicken with Sweet Chili Sauce

When you shop in an Asian market for Thai fish sauce, you may be tempted to buy a bottled Sweet Chili Sauce as well. Though it would save time, nothing beats this fruity sauce to complement the zingy Thai chicken.

3 tablespoons Thai fish sauce
2 serrano chiles, seeded and minced
3 tablespoons minced garlic
1 tablespoon minced cilantro stems
1 tablespoon sugar
1 teaspoon curry powder
$^1/_2$ teaspoon *each* pepper and turmeric
8 chicken thighs (about 2$^1/_2$ pounds)

Sweet Chili Sauce:
$^3/_4$ cup golden raisins
1 medium tomato, peeled and quartered
3 cloves garlic, minced
1 serrano chile, seeded and chopped
$^1/_4$ teaspoon salt
$^1/_2$ cup *each* plum jam and orange juice
2 tablespoons packed brown sugar
3 tablespoons rice vinegar
1 teaspoon crushed red pepper

Combine fish sauce, chiles, garlic, cilantro stems, sugar, curry powder, pepper, and turmeric in a large bowl. Add chicken and turn to coat. Cover and refrigerate 4 hours.

Prepare sauce: In a food processor, whirl raisins, tomato, garlic, chile, and salt to make a coarse purée. In a 2-quart pan, heat jam, orange juice, brown sugar, vinegar, and red pepper over low heat until jam melts. Add raisin mixture; simmer, uncovered, on medium heat 20 minutes. Reduce heat to low; cook, stirring, until sauce thickens. Let cool.

Place chicken in a shallow baking pan, leaving 1-inch space between each piece. Bake, uncovered, in a 375° oven until meat near bone is no longer pink when cut, 40 to 50 minutes. Serve with Sweet Chili Sauce.

Makes 4 to 6 servings

Some folks love hot and spicy food; others have trouble with the slightest heat from chiles.

To dampen the "fire," squeeze lime juice over the spiced food.

Even though it's not a normal part of the seasoning, the lime juice adds an exotic flavor while cooling the heat.

Chicken Potato Stacks

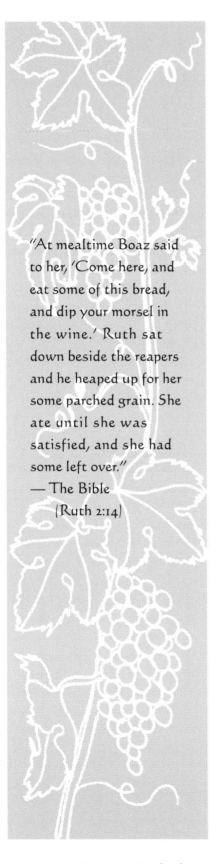

This recipe serves four but can easily be doubled or tripled; just add one more piece of chicken and potato per serving. If you increase the recipe, place the chicken in two baking pans, leaving space between each serving. Crowding pieces creates steam and soggy potatoes. Use only 1½ teaspoons of oil per potato to keep the potatos crisp, not greasy.

4 red, thin-skinned potatoes,
   5 ounces each
2 tablespoons olive oil
½ teaspoon salt
4 boneless, skinless chicken breast
   halves, 5 ounces each
2 tablespoons Dijon mustard
2 teaspoons Italian seasoning
Garlic salt
Pepper
Paprika

In a pan, boil unpeeled potatoes, covered, in 2 inches of water until barely tender, 15 to 20 minutes. Drain; let cool. Peel potatoes; using large holes on a shredder, grate potatoes lengthwise to make long shreds. Place in a large bowl with oil and salt. Toss to separate shreds and evenly coat with oil.

Place breasts in greased, shallow baking pan, leaving 2 inches between each. Spread 1½ teaspoons mustard over each breast; sprinkle each with ½ teaspoon Italian seasoning (or any of your favorite herbs) and garlic salt and pepper to taste. Completely cover each breast with ¼ of potato mixture; dust tops with paprika. If made ahead, cover and refrigerate up to 8 hours.

Preheat oven to 425°. Bake chicken for 20 minutes; broil 3 to 4 inches from heat for 2 minutes or until potatoes are golden brown.

Makes 4 servings

Chicken & Bulgur Casserole

The appealing colors of the golden squash, bright green herb garnish, and brown-black currants also make this easy family meal a fresh choice for a potluck dinner.

1¼ pounds boneless, skinless chicken thighs
½ teaspoon *each* ground cinnamon, allspice, and paprika
¼ teaspoon *each* salt and pepper
1 tablespoon vegetable oil
1 medium onion, chopped
¼ cup water
1 cup bulgur (cracked wheat)
1½ cups diced butternut squash, cut into ½-inch cubes
⅓ cup dried currants
1½ teaspoons grated orange peel
2½ cups chicken broth
1 tablespoon *each* chopped parsley and fresh mint leaves

Cut thighs into pieces about 2 inches square. Combine cinnamon, allspice, paprika, salt, and pepper; sprinkle over chicken. Heat oil in a wide frying pan over medium-high heat. Add chicken and cook until lightly browned, 2 to 3 minutes per side. Lift out and set aside.

Add onion and water to pan. Simmer, covered, over low heat until liquid evaporates, 4 to 5 minutes. Remove pan from heat; stir in bulgur, squash, currants, and orange peel.

Grease a 9 by 13-inch baking pan. Evenly spread bulgur mixture in pan; arrange chicken on top. Heat broth to boiling; pour into pan. Cover pan tightly with foil. Bake in a 350° oven 45 minutes or until squash is tender and all liquid is absorbed. Sprinkle with parsley and mint.

Makes 4 servings

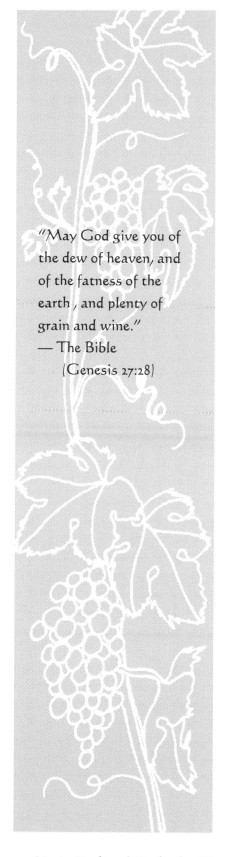

"May God give you of the dew of heaven, and of the fatness of the earth , and plenty of grain and wine."
— The Bible
(Genesis 27:28)

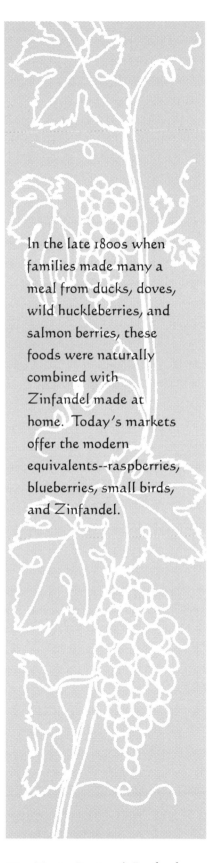

In the late 1800s when families made many a meal from ducks, doves, wild huckleberries, and salmon berries, these foods were naturally combined with Zinfandel made at home. Today's markets offer the modern equivalents--raspberries, blueberries, small birds, and Zinfandel.

Berry–browned Quail or Game Hens

Though Zinfandel is a dry wine, its berry flavors and apparent sweetness pair beautifully with the poultry's raspberry marinade. After cooking, the flesh of the bird stays white, but the ruby red marinade turns the skin a rich mahogany color.

8 quail or 4 Rock Cornish game hens
2 cups raspberries
1/4 cup Zinfandel
2 tablespoons olive oil
1 teaspoon Dijon mustard
1 teaspoon sugar
1 teaspoon dried thyme leaves
1/2 teaspoon salt
1/2 teaspoon cracked black pepper

Cut through breastbone of each quail with poultry shears; spread quail open, skin side up, on a flat surface and press firmly to crack bones. If using game hens, cut through breastbone of each; cut out rest of backbone with poultry shears. Place birds in a heavy plastic bag.

Purée raspberries in a food processor; push purée through a sieve to remove seeds. Add wine, oil, mustard, sugar, thyme, salt, and pepper to purée; whisk until smooth. Pour over birds and seal bag. Refrigerate 8 to 24 hours.

Preheat oven to 400°. Drain marinade into a bowl and reserve. Place birds, skin side up, on rack in a shallow roasting pan. Roast quail until breast meat is cooked through but still pink near bone, 8 to 10 minutes. Roast game hens until meat near thighbone is no longer pink, 30 to 40 minutes. Brush birds with reserved marinade twice during the last half of cooking.

Makes 4 servings

Potlatch Salmon

When Indians from the Pacific Northwest put on a potlatch to impress friends and enemies with their wealth and power, whole salmon were wrapped in seaweed and cooked in a pit with corn and shellfish. You can get the same moist results by wrapping fish in fresh cornhusks and baking. For best results, use a center-cut fillet section of fish.

 4 ears corn in the husk
 4 pieces salmon fillet, 4 to 5 ounces
   each, cut ³/₄-inch thick, skin removed
Salt and pepper
 2 tablespoons butter
¹/₄ cup chopped red bell pepper,
¹/₄ cup chicken broth
 2 green onions with tops, thinly sliced
¹/₄ cup canned diced green chiles
¹/₄ teaspoon ground cumin
 1 large tomato, peeled, seeded, and diced
 1 tablespoon coarsely chopped cilantro

Husk corn: Leaving husks attached at stem ends, peel back to expose corn. Cut off corn cobs with a sharp knife and rinse husks.

Season fish with salt and pepper. Place 1 piece of fish in each husk; smooth husk over fish and tie open end with a thin strip of husk. Place packets on baking sheet. Refrigerate until ready to bake.

With a knife, cut kernels from corn cobs. Melt butter in a 2-quart pan over medium heat. Add corn, bell pepper, and broth; cover and simmer 5 minutes. Add green onions, chiles, and cumin. Simmer 2 minutes; set aside.

Preheat oven to 400°. Bake packets, uncovered, 20 minutes or until fish loses wet look and begins to flake (open packet with tip of knife to check). Simmer corn mixture, uncovered, until heated through and liquid evaporates. Add tomato and cilantro; cook for 1 minute. Add salt and pepper to taste. Place salmon on individual plates. Open husks and top servings with warm corn salsa.

Makes 4 servings

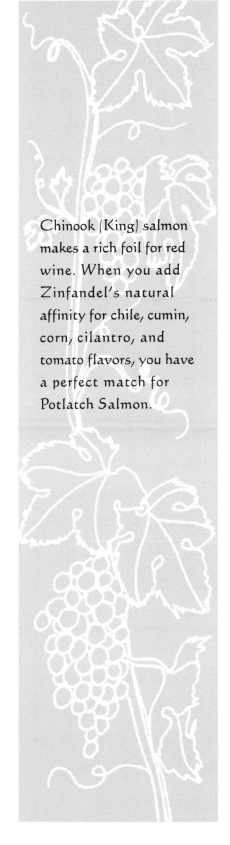

Chinook (King) salmon makes a rich foil for red wine. When you add Zinfandel's natural affinity for chile, cumin, corn, cilantro, and tomato flavors, you have a perfect match for Potlatch Salmon.

Hangtown Fry

First whipped up in Placerville, California (known as Hangtown in Gold Rush days), this egg and oyster dish was created to satisfy the tastes of a miner who struck it rich. Since eggs sold for around 50 cents apiece and bacon and oysters were worth more than gold, such a meal cost $6 to $7, a fortune in those days. The recipe can be doubled or tripled, but it's easier to make individual omelets.

2 large eggs
1 tablespoon milk
1/4 teaspoon salt
Dash of pepper
1/8 teaspoon ground nutmeg
1/3 cup oysters
All-purpose flour
1 tablespoon butter
1 tablespoon chopped parsley
3 strips crisply fried bacon or
    browned link sausages

Break eggs into a small bowl and add milk, salt, pepper, and nutmeg. Beat with a fork just enough to mix yolks and whites.

Cut oysters in half, if large; leave small ones whole. Dust oysters with flour. Melt butter in a 7- to 8-inch nonstick frying pan over medium-high heat. Add oysters and cook for 30 seconds on each side.

Pour egg mixture into pan. As eggs begin to set around edges, lift edges and let uncooked egg flow underneath. When eggs no longer flow freely, run a spatula around edge of omelet and flip onto a plate, bottom side up. Sprinkle with parsley and garnish with bacon or sausages.

Makes 1 serving

In 49er gold-mining camps, Hangtown Fry was a one-skillet meal for hungry miners with plenty of gold.

As soon as bacon began to fry, oysters would be dropped into a pan. After a quick stir, eggs would be added. One quick flip completed the cooking, creating an historic meal that might have been the first "California cuisine."

Deviled Cracked Crab

It's hard to stop eating this dish once your fingers are covered with sauce. When the last bite of sweet crab is gone and the last piece of garlicky bread is dunked in the spicy sauce, you may want to pass a basket of hot, damp cloths around the table.

2 tablespoons olive oil
1 large onion, chopped
4 stalks celery, chopped
3 cloves garlic, minced
1 can (10½ ounces) beef consommé
1 can (8 ounces) tomato sauce
3 tablespoons Worcestershire sauce
4 black peppercorns
¼ teaspoon crushed red pepper
1 bay leaf
2 sprigs parsley
2 Dungeness crab, cooked and cleaned
Garlic bread

Heat oil in an 8-quart pot over medium heat. Add onion, celery, and garlic. Cook over medium heat, stirring frequently, until onion is soft but not browned. Add consommé, tomato sauce, Worcestershire, peppercorns, red pepper, bay leaf, and parsley. Bring to a boil; reduce heat, cover, and simmer 30 minutes. Strain sauce and discard seasonings; return sauce to pan.

Cut crab bodies into quarters. Crack legs and claws so sauce will penetrate meat. Add crab to sauce; cover and simmer 30 minutes.

Lift out crab and place in a wide serving bowl. Pour sauce into small side bowls for dunking garlic bread.

Makes 4 servings

Contrary to popular opinion, shellfish and red wine do go together.

Zinfandel is a grand match for this spicy crab feast.

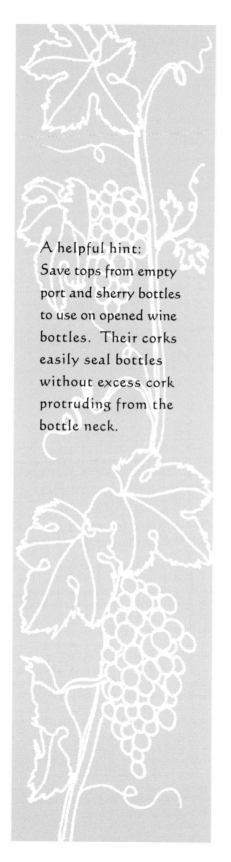

Five–Minute Shrimp

When it comes to shrimp cookery, we're partial to this stir-fry. It's simple, speedy, and—because it's laced with garlic and ginger—deliciously pungent.

1 pound medium shrimp, shelled and deveined
2 teaspoons cornstarch
$\frac{1}{2}$ teaspoon sesame oil
$\frac{1}{4}$ teaspoon salt
Dash of white pepper

Spicy Sauce:
$\frac{1}{4}$ cup chicken broth
2 tablespoons catsup
1 tablespoon Worcestershire sauce
1 tablespoon brandy
$\frac{1}{2}$ teaspoon Dijon mustard
$1\frac{1}{2}$ teaspoons cornstarch

2 tablespoons vegetable oil
3 cloves garlic, minced
2 teaspoons minced ginger
4 green onions with tops, thinly sliced

In a medium bowl, toss shrimp with cornstarch, sesame oil, salt, and pepper; let stand 15 minutes.

Combine spicy sauce ingredients in a small bowl.

Heat vegetable oil in a wok or wide frying pan over high heat until hot. Add garlic and ginger and stir-fry for 10 seconds. Add shrimp and stir-fry until pink, 2 to 3 minutes. Add green onions and stir once. Stir sauce once, add to pan, and cook, stirring, until sauce bubbles and thickens.

Makes 4 servings

Pasta, Pizza & Grains

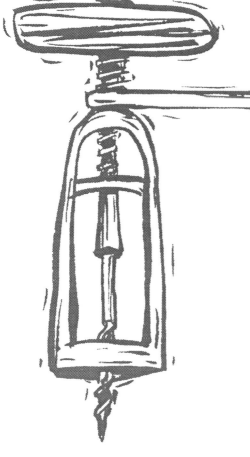

Italian "Coffee-Grinder" corkscrew 18th century

Never have pasta, pizza, and grains been so popular. Once today's health-conscious folks became aware of their comforting and nourishing qualities, these sturdy foods quickly became the entrées and side dishes of choice.

This chapter showcases recipes for wide range of pastas, from festive Fettucine with Shrimp & Olives to Old-Fashioned Macaroni & Cheese. A basic dough makes it easy to tailor pizza toppings and calzone fillings to your family's taste. And you can build a menu around such offerings as Sun-dried Tomato Risotto or Couscous & Vegetable Ragout.

Fettuccine with Shrimp & Olives

With all the colors of the Italian flag (red, green, and white), this full-meal pasta makes an attractive and tempting entrée for guests. The sauce cooks quickly, keeping flavors fresh.

  2 tablespoons olive oil
  1 small onion, chopped
  2 cloves garlic, minced
  2 ounces sliced pepperoni, cut into slivers
  1/4 pound mushrooms, sliced
  1 tablespoon anchovy paste
  1 can (14 1/2 ounces) diced tomatoes, undrained
  1 can (8 ounces) tomato sauce
  1 can (4 ounces) sliced ripe olives
  1/4 teaspoon *each* dried oregano and crushed red pepper
  3/4 pound small cooked shrimp
  12 ounces fettuccine
  2 tablespoons chopped flat-leaf parsley

Heat oil in a deep frying pan over medium heat. Add onion; cover and cook, stirring once or twice, for 5 minutes. Add garlic, pepperoni, and mushrooms.

Cook, uncovered, stirring occasionally, until mushrooms are lightly browned. Stir in anchovy paste. Add tomatoes, tomato sauce, olives, oregano, and red pepper. Bring to a boil; reduce heat and simmer, uncovered, for 10 minutes. Stir in shrimp and heat through.

In a large kettle of boiling water, cook pasta until tender but firm to bite, 8 to 10 minutes; drain. Place in a serving bowl. Add sauce, toss gently, and sprinkle with parsley.

Makes 6 servings

Pasta with Artichoke Sauce

In the time it takes to cook the pasta or tortellini, you can whip up this luscious white sauce. Rich and creamy, like traditional Alfredo-style sauce made with whipping cream, it contains far fewer calories and less fat. Buy light cream cheese in a foil-wrapped brick, not in a plastic tub. To add color and texture to the meal, serve pasta with a crisp green salad and Zinfandel.

1 tablespoon butter
2 cloves garlic, minced
1 cup chicken broth
1 package (8 ounces) Neufchâtel or light cream cheese, cut into chunks
1/2 cup (1 1/2 ounces) shredded dry jack cheese
1 can (14 ounces) artichoke hearts packed in water, drained and quartered lengthwise, or 1 package (10 ounces) frozen artichoke hearts, cooked and drained
1/2 teaspoon dried Italian seasoning
2 tablespoons chopped parsley
Cracked black pepper
8 ounces dried penne or fusilli pasta or fresh tortellini

Melt butter in a 2-quart pan over medium-low heat. Add garlic and cook, stirring, until golden, about 2 minutes. Add broth and Neufchâtel cheese. Heat to simmering; whisk to smoothly blend cheese. Add dry jack cheese and stir until it melts. Add artichoke hearts, Italian seasoning, parsley, and pepper to taste; heat through.

In a large kettle of boiling water, cook dried pasta until tender but firm to bite, 8 to 10 minutes, or cook fresh tortellini according to package direction. Drain. Place pasta in a serving bowl. Add sauce and toss gently.

Makes 4 servings

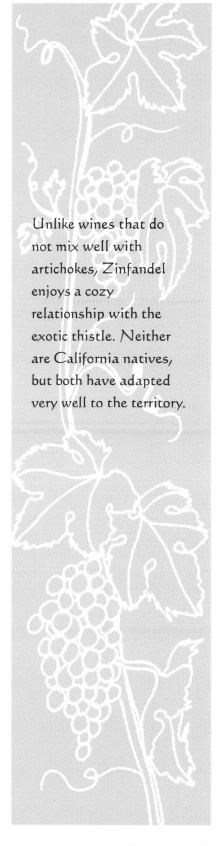

Unlike wines that do not mix well with artichokes, Zinfandel enjoys a cozy relationship with the exotic thistle. Neither are California natives, but both have adapted very well to the territory.

Fettuccine & Sweet Peppers

A festival of taste, this midsummer pasta features juicy, sun-ripened tomatoes, red and yellow peppers, and fresh basil. None of the flavor is lost as the peppers are cooked only until tender and the tomatoes are tossed in at the last minute and just heated through.

> 1/2 tablespoon butter
> 1/4 cup pine nuts
> 2 tablespoons olive oil
> 1 *each* red and yellow bell pepper
>   (1 pound total), seeded, cut in half
>   crosswise, and cut lengthwise into
>   1/4-inch strips
> 2 cloves garlic, minced
> 2 medium tomatoes, diced
> 8 ounces spinach fettuccine
> 2 tablespoons shredded fresh basil
> 1/2 cup grated Parmesan cheese

Melt butter in a small pan over medium heat. Add nuts and cook, shaking pan often, until nuts are golden brown, 3 to 4 minutes. Set aside.

Heat oil in a wide frying pan over medium-high heat. Add peppers and garlic and cook for 1 minute. Cover pan and cook, stirring once or twice, until peppers are just barely tender, 6 to 8 minutes. Add tomatoes and cook for 1 minute to heat through.

In a large kettle of boiling water, cook pasta until tender but firm to bite, 8 to 10 minutes; drain. Place in a serving bowl. Add peppers and tomatoes, basil, and nuts. Toss gently. Add half of the cheese and toss.

Sprinkle remaining cheese over the top.

Makes 4 servings

An opened bottle of red Zinfandel keeps for 4 or 5 days at serving temperature. It loses its flavor faster when refrigerated because cooling and rewarming cause the wine to oxidize.

White or Rosé Zinfandel needs to be refrigerated. An open bottle will keep for about a week.

Linguine with Salami & Mushrooms

Popular pizza toppings, mushrooms and salami, are also delicious in pasta sauce. This tasty dish is easy to whip up for a quick meal for family or unexpected guests.

- 2 tablespoons olive oil
- 1/2 pound mushrooms, thinly sliced
- 4 ounces salami, cut into matchstick-size strips
- 3 green onions, thinly sliced
- 1 can (14 1/2 ounces) diced tomatoes, undrained
- 1/2 cup whipping cream
- Cracked black pepper
- 8 ounces linguine

Heat oil in a wide frying pan over medium heat. Add mushrooms and salami and cook, stirring occasionally, until mushrooms are lightly browned, 4 to 5 minutes. Add green onions and cook 1 minute. Add tomatoes and cook until mushrooms are tender and most of the tomato liquid has evaporated, 4 to 5 minutes. Stir in cream and pepper to taste; heat through.

In a large kettle of boiling water, cook pasta until tender but firm to bite, 8 to 10 minutes; drain. Place in a serving bowl. Add sauce and toss.

Makes 4 servings

A good bottle of Zinfandel for an everyday meal will cost under $10. Serve your more complex—and more expensive—Zins at company dinners. Prices will run between $12 and $30 per bottle.

Porcini Mushroom Lasagne

*Here is a recipe for guests and family
members who are vegetarians. Sun-dried
tomatoes, porcini mushrooms, and flavorful
cheeses set off taste buds, preparing them
for the contrast of Zinfandel. Lasagne for
some, steak for others, Zinfandel for all.*

Bechamel Sauce:
   6 tablespoons butter
   6 tablespoons all-purpose flour
  $1/2$ teaspoon salt
  $1/2$ teaspoon white pepper
  $1/4$ teaspoon ground nutmeg
   4 cups milk, heated to simmering

   2 ounces dried porcini mushrooms
   2 ounces dried sun-dried tomatoes or
      1 cup sun-dried tomatoes marinated
      in oil, drained
   2 tablespoons butter
   1 cup chopped cooked spinach,
      squeezed dry
   8 ounces ricotta cheese
Salt and pepper
10 ounces dried lasagne noodles
   2 cups freshly grated Parmesan cheese

Prepare sauce: Melt butter in a 2-quart pan
over medium heat. Add flour, salt, pepper,
and nutmeg and cook, stirring, for 1 minute.
Gradually stir in milk; cook, stirring, until
sauce boils and thickens. Place a piece of
plastic film on sauce to prevent skin from
forming and set sauce aside.

Cook vegetables before
adding wine to a stew.
The acids in wine may
harden vegetables such
as potatoes and carrots.

When cooking meat,
add wine; the acids
tenderize meat. Precook
vegetables separately on
the stove, or in a
microwave oven, before
adding to the stew.

In separate bowls, cover mushrooms and sun-dried tomatoes with warm water and let soak 20 minutes; drain. (If using tomatoes packed in oil, do not soak.) Rinse mushrooms to remove any grit. Coarsely chop mushrooms and tomatoes.

Melt butter in a wide frying pan over medium heat. Add mushrooms, tomatoes, and spinach; cook for 3 minutes. Remove from heat and let cool. Mix with ricotta cheese and salt and pepper to taste.

In a large kettle of boiling water, cook noodles until tender but firm to bite, 10 to 12 minutes. Drain, rinse with cold water, and drain again.

Grease a 9 by 13-inch baking dish. Spread a thin layer of sauce over the bottom. Arrange ⅓ of noodles in an even layer over sauce. Spread ⅓ of spinach mixture over noodles, top with ⅓ of sauce, then sprinkle with ⅓ of Parmesan cheese. Repeat layering two more times, ending with Parmesan cheese. If made ahead, cover and refrigerate up to 24 hours.

Bake, covered, in a 350° oven for 30 minutes. Uncover and bake 10 to 20 more minutes or until hot and bubbly. Let stand 10 minutes, then cut into squares to serve.

Makes 8 servings

Old–Fashioned Macaroni & Cheese

In these days of instant cooking, it's nice to find a homey dish that has never gone out of style, just been overlooked by clock watchers. Choose your cheese: Fontina imparts a nutty flavor; Cheddar adds bite and an orange color. The crumb topping makes a crunchy contrast to the creamy sauce.

$1^{1}/_{2}$ tablespoons butter
$1^{1}/_{2}$ tablespoons all-purpose flour
$^{1}/_{4}$ teaspoon dry mustard
$^{1}/_{8}$ teaspoon ground nutmeg
$1^{1}/_{2}$ cups milk, heated to simmering
$1^{1}/_{2}$ cups (6 ounces) shredded Fontina
   or Cheddar cheese
$^{1}/_{4}$ cup grated Parmesan cheese
Salt and pepper
8 ounces medium-size elbow macaroni
1 cup fresh sourdough bread crumbs
2 tablespoons melted butter

Melt $1^{1}/_{2}$ tablespoons butter in a 2-quart pan over medium heat. Add flour, mustard, and nutmeg and cook, stirring, for 1 minute. Gradually stir in milk; cook, stirring, until sauce boils and thickens slightly. Remove pan from heat and stir in cheeses and salt and pepper to taste. (Cheese will not melt completely until baked.)

In a large kettle of boiling water, cook macaroni until tender but firm to bite, 8 to 10 minutes. Drain, rinse with cold water, and drain again. Combine macaroni and cheese mixture; pour into a greased $1^{1}/_{2}$-quart casserole. Toss bread crumbs with melted butter; sprinkle evenly over macaroni. If made ahead, cover and refrigerate up to 24 hours.

Bake, uncovered, in a 350° oven until bubbly and lightly browned, 30 to 40 minutes.

Makes 4 to 6 servings

Crispy Pizza Dough

The secret to good homemade pizza is to bake it in a very hot oven. This recipe turns out pizza with a crisp crust and a chewy interior. If you don't use all the dough in one baking, cut it in half, shape each half into a disk, wrap the disks in plastic, and refrigerate until the next day or freeze for later use. Defrost frozen dough before using; bring both refrigerated and thawed dough to room temperature before rolling it out.

1   package (¹/₄ ounce) active dry yeast
¹/₄ cup warm water (110°)
3   cups all-purpose flour
1   teaspoon salt
1   teaspoon *each* dried oregano and
     basil
³/₄ cup cool water
1   tablespoon honey
2   tablespoons olive oil

In a small bowl, combine yeast and warm water; let stand 10 minutes until foamy. Combine flour, salt, oregano, and basil in a large bowl. Combine cool water, honey, and oil in a small bowl.

Make a well in center of dry ingredients; add dissolved yeast and honey mixtures. Mix well. Turn dough onto a floured surface and knead until smooth and elastic, 8 to 10 minutes. Place dough in a greased bowl and turn to coat. Cover bowl with a towel; let rise in a warm place for 1 hour or until dough doubles in size. Proceed with pizza toppings (page 70) or calzone filling (page 71).

To make dough in a food processor, process flour, salt, basil, and oregano 10 seconds. With processor running, pour honey mixture down feed tube, then pour dissolved yeast down feed tube. Process until mixture forms a ball. Turn dough onto a floured surface and knead until smooth and elastic, 4 to 5 minutes.

Makes 2 12-inch pizzas or 6 calzone

Tired of cooking? Don't despair. Food industry marketing experts say fast food is the wave of the future.

They predict we'll see a microwave in every car and individual food packages at every meal.

Nothing compares with fresh pizza dough. When time is short, however, you can still enjoy a great pizza by matching these toppings with thawed frozen bread dough or Italian bread shells—prebaked, refrigerated, or frozen.

Sweet Onion Pizza

Onions and nuts give this topping a buttery sweetness.

> $^1/_2$ recipe Crispy Pizza Dough (page 69)
> Olive oil
> Caramelized onions (page 86)
> $^1/_4$ cup pine nuts
> $1^1/_2$ cups (6 ounces) shredded
>   Gouda cheese

Preheat oven to 450°. Roll out or stretch pizza dough into a 12-inch circle; turn up edges to form a rim. Place dough in a greased 12-inch pizza pan; brush edges of dough lightly with oil. Leaving a $^1/_2$-inch border all around, spread onions over dough. Top with pine nuts; sprinkle cheese over nuts.

Bake 15 to 18 minutes or until cheese melts and crust is crisp and browned. Slide pizza onto a warm plate and cut into wedges.

Makes 4 to 6 servings

Tomato & Pesto Pizza

A taste of Italy–tomatoes and olives combine with pesto for a flavor-filled topping.

> $^1/_2$ recipe Crispy Pizza Dough (page 69)
> Olive oil
> $^1/_2$ cup Pesto (page 87)
> 4 Roma tomatoes, sliced $^1/_4$-inch-thick
> $^1/_4$ cup oil-cured olives, pitted and
>   chopped
> Freshly ground pepper

Preheat oven to 450°. Prepare pizza dough as directed in recipe above. Brush edges of dough lightly with oil. Leaving a $^1/_2$-inch border all around, spread pesto over dough. Place tomatoes in a single layer over pesto. Sprinkle with olives. Lightly brush tomatoes with oil; season with pepper.

Bake 15 to 18 minutes or until crust is crisp and browned. Slide pizza onto a warm plate and cut into wedges.

Makes 4 to 6 servings

Mixed Greens Calzone

*Calzone might be called "pizza to go."
Because the dough is wrapped around a
savory filling, it resembles a turnover. This
one is redolent with Middle Eastern spices.
Enjoy calzone at home or slip in a pack for
a hike or bike ride.*

     1 pound Swiss chard
     4 large leeks (2 inches in diameter)
     2 tablespoons olive oil
     2 cloves garlic, minced
    1/2 cup chopped parsley
    1/2 teaspoon *each* salt and dried mint
    1/4 teaspoon *each* ground cinnamon
        and pepper
    1 1/2 cups (6 ounces) shredded Jarlsburg
        cheese
    Crispy Pizza Dough (page 69)

Finely chop chard stems; coarsely chop
leaves. Thinly slice tender white part of
leeks.

Heat oil in a 5-quart kettle over medium
heat. Add chard stems, leeks, and garlic;
cook 10 minutes. Add chard leaves, parsley,
salt, mint, cinnamon, and pepper; mix well.
Cook, covered, for 10 minutes or until
greens are tender. Uncover and continue to
cook until all liquid has evaporated. Let
cool. Stir in cheese.

Preheat oven to 450°. Divide pizza dough
into 6 equal pieces. To make each calzone,
roll 1 piece of dough into a 7-inch circle on
a floured board. Place 1/2 cup filling on half
of circle, 1 inch from edge. Moisten edge
of dough with water, fold dough over to
make a half moon, and press edge to seal.
Fold edge of dough up onto itself to form a
curl, pinching edge as you curl. Place on
greased baking sheets. Bake 10 to 12
minutes or until golden brown. Serve hot
or a room temperature.

Makes 6 calzone

"What through youth
gave love and roses,
Age still leaves us
friends and wine."
—Thomas Moore
(1779-1852)

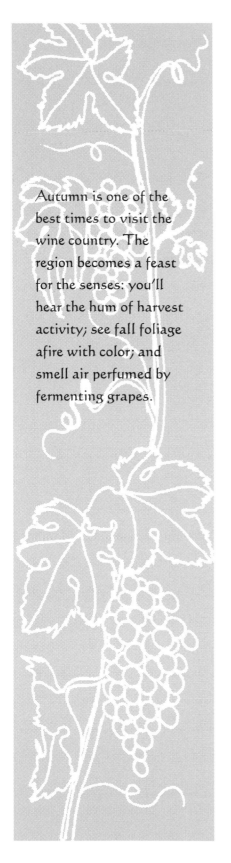

Sun–dried Tomato Risotto

Risotto shines as a first course and makes a perfect partner for grilled or roasted meats. Our shortened method of making risotto may differ from the traditional Italian technique, but loses nothing in the process. Adding cooking broth all at once, rather than in the usual ½ cup increments, and simmering the rice uncovered gives risotto its characteristic creamy texture.

- 1 tablespoon butter
- 2 tablespoons oil from sun-dried tomatoes or olive oil
- 1 medium onion, chopped
- 2 cloves garlic, minced
- 1½ cups short-grain rice, such as Italian aborio or California pearl rice
- 4½ cups chicken broth
- ¼ cup sun-dried tomatoes, marinated in oil
- ¼ cup grated Parmesan cheese
- 2 tablespoons chopped flat-leaf parsley
- 2 tablespoons chopped fresh basil

Melt butter with oil in a 3-quart pan over medium heat. Add onion and cook, stirring occasionally, until onion is soft and golden, 4 to 5 minutes. Add garlic and rice and stir until rice is opaque, 3 to 4 minutes.

Add broth. Cook, stirring frequently, until broth comes to a boil. Adjust heat so rice boils gently; cook, uncovered, until rice is tender yet firm and most of liquid is absorbed, 20 to 22 minutes.

Turn off heat and stir in sun-dried tomatoes, cheese, parsley, and basil. Serve at once or cover pan and keep risotto warm up to 15 minutes.

Makes 6 servings

Wild & Brown Rice Pilaf

Nuts, vegetables, and a blend of wild and brown rice make a nutritious, delicious, and filling side dish to enjoy with meat.

> 2/3 cup (4 ounces) wild rice
> 1/3 cup brown rice
> 3 tablespoons butter
> 1/3 cup *each* finely diced onion, carrot, and celery
> 1 can (14½ ounces) beef broth
> 2 cups water
> 1/4 teaspoon rubbed sage
> 1/4 teaspoon pepper
> 1/2 cup chopped pecans or slivered almonds

Wash wild and brown rice together in water; drain. Melt 2 tablespoons of the butter in a 2- to 3-quart, heat-proof casserole over medium heat. Add onion, carrot, and celery and cook, stirring frequently, until onion is soft and golden, 4 to 5 minutes. Add wild and brown rice, broth, water, sage, and pepper; heat to boiling.

Cover casserole and bake in a 350° oven until rices are tender and liquid is absorbed, 1½ to 1¾ hours.

Meanwhile, melt remaining 1 tablespoon butter in a pan over medium heat. Stir in nuts and cook, shaking pan often, until nuts are golden brown. Just before serving, stir nuts into hot rice.

Makes 4 to 6 servings

When traveling through the wine country in autumn, it's fun to try and identify different varieties of grapes by the colors of their foliage.

White wine grape leaves turn gold, while the leaves of Zinfandel and other red varieties acquire a reddish tinge. Older, head-pruned Zinfandel vineyards have fewer vines. Their foliage may become crimson.

Fruited Rice Pilaf

The fruity flavor and sweet-tart taste of this rice dish make it a favorite to accompany lamb shish kebab, roast chicken, and pork entrées.

$^1/_4$ cup raisins
$^1/_4$ cup dried apricots, chopped
2 tablespoons Zinfandel
2 tablespoons butter
1 cup uncooked long-grain white rice
1 can (14$^1/_2$ ounces) chicken broth
1 cinnamon stick
3 whole cloves
$^1/_4$ cup roasted cashews, coarsely chopped

Place raisins, apricots, and wine in a small pan. Cover and place over low heat until simmering. Remove from heat and set aside.

Melt butter in a 2-quart pan over medium heat. Add rice and cook, stirring, for 2 minutes or until rice is lightly toasted. Add broth, cinnamon stick, and cloves. Bring to a boil. Cover; reduce heat and simmer 20 minutes or until rice is tender and liquid is absorbed.

Discard cinnamon stick and cloves. Fluff rice with a fork. Add raisins, apricots, and nuts and toss gently. Cover and let stand 5 minutes before serving.

Makes 4 to 6 servings

To winemakers, there is no better combination than lamb and Zinfandel. In addition to producing good Zinfandel, Sonoma and Amador Counties both boast of their lamb.

The secret to buying good lamb is to select a butcher who hangs the meat long enough for flavor to develop.

Rice Pilaf with Avocado

This tasty rice dish can hold its own with steak, grilled sausages, and hot, spicy Mexican food. Adding avocado gives the pilaf a pleasant butter quality.

- 2 tablespoons butter
- 1 small onion, finely chopped
- 1 clove garlic, minced
- $\frac{1}{2}$ cup chopped, peeled fresh or canned tomatoes
- 1 cup uncooked long-grain white rice
- $\frac{1}{4}$ teaspoon *each* ground cumin and dried oregano
- 1 can (14$\frac{1}{2}$ ounces) chicken broth
- 1 small avocado

Heat butter in a 2-quart pan over medium heat. Add onion and cook, stirring once or twice, until onion is soft but not brown, 4 to 5 minutes. Add garlic, tomatoes, and rice; cook, stirring constantly, for 2 minutes or until rice is opaque.

Stir in cumin and oregano; add broth. Bring to a boil; cover, reduce heat, and simmer 20 minutes or until rice is tender and liquid is absorbed. Turn off heat.

Peel and pit avocado; cut into $\frac{1}{2}$-inch cubes. Fluff rice with a fork; add avocado and toss gently. Cover and let stand 5 minutes before serving.

Makes 4 to 6 servings

To ripen an avocado, place it in a paper bag with an apple. Close the bag and store it at room temperature. Check daily for ripeness.

Once ripe, avocados may be stored in the refrigerator. If you store a cut avocado, leave the pit in to keep it from turning brown.

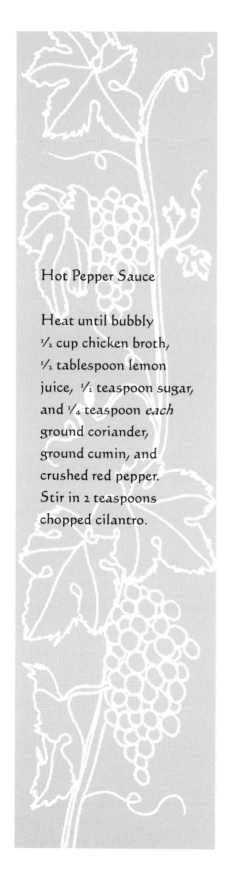

Hot Pepper Sauce

Heat until bubbly
½ cup chicken broth,
½ tablespoon lemon
juice, ½ teaspoon sugar,
and ¼ teaspoon *each*
ground coriander,
ground cumin, and
crushed red pepper.
Stir in 2 teaspoons
chopped cilantro.

Couscous & Vegetable Ragout

*When you want a meatless meal that looks
festive and tastes terrific, try this Moroccan-
influenced ragout.*

> 2 tablespoons olive oil
> 1 large onion, cut into 1-inch cubes
> 1 red bell pepper, seeded and cut
>   into 1-inch squares
> ½ teaspoon *each* ground ginger,
>   turmeric, black pepper, and paprika
> 3 medium carrots, sliced ½-inch-thick
> 1 large thin-skinned potato, cut into
>   chunks
> 1 sweet potato, cut into chunks
> 2 medium tomatoes, peeled and diced
> 1 cup chicken broth
> ¼ cup catsup
> ½ teaspoon salt
> 1 can (15 ounces) garbanzos, drained
> 2 small zucchini, sliced ½-inch-thick
> 2 crookneck squash, cut into chunks
> 2 cups couscous
> ¼ cup currants
> ⅛ teaspoon ground cinnamon
> ¼ cup slivered almonds, toasted
> 2 tablespoons chopped cilantro
>   Hot Pepper Sauce (recipe at left)

Heat oil in a 5-quart pan over medium-low
heat. Add onion, cover, and cook 5 minutes.
Add bell pepper, ginger, turmeric, pepper, and
paprika; cook, uncovered, for 2 minutes. Add
carrots, potato, sweet potato, tomatoes,
broth, catsup, and salt. Mix well. Bring to a
boil; cover, reduce heat, and simmer 20
minutes. Stir in garbanzos, zucchini, and
crookneck squash; cover and simmer until
vegetables are tender, 10 to 15 minutes.

Cook couscous according to package
directions, adding currants and cinnamon to
cooking liquid. Spread couscous on a serving
platter. Lift out vegetables with a slotted
spoon and mound in center. Sprinkle with
almonds and cilantro. Pour cooking broth
into a small pitcher. Pass Hot Pepper Sauce
and broth separately to pour over couscous.

Makes 6 servings

Salads & Vegetables

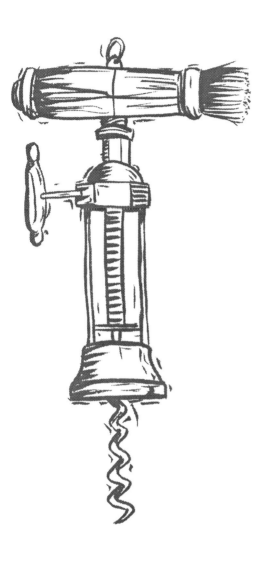

Antique corkscrew with built-in brush

A pristine green salad with a well-balanced vinaigrette dressing can be difficult to pair with any wine, but there are ways to change the flavor profile of the dressing to make it more compatible. All of our selections are created especially with Zin in mind. You'll find salads to introduce or end a meal, accompany an entrée, or even act as the main course.

Artichokes, onions, potatoes, tomatoes, eggplant, and beans —our delicious side dishes take advantage of the bounty of fresh vegetables available in gardens and at farmers' markets.

Zinfandel Vinaigrette

When salad introduces a meal, some chefs prefer to delay wine service until the following course. But there's no need to wait when you toss leafy greens with this wine-friendly dressing.

> 1/4 cup *each* olive oil and vegetable oil
> 2 tablespoons Zinfandel
> 2 tablespoons red wine vinegar
> 1 tablespoon minced shallots
> 1 teaspoon Dijon mustard
> 1 teaspoon sugar
> 1/4 teaspoon salt
> Dash of black pepper

In a jar, combine all ingredients; shake to mix thoroughly. Use at once or refrigerate up to 1 week. Shake again before adding to a salad.

Makes 3/4 cup dressing

Creamy Soy Dressing

This mayonnaise-based dressing adds a new dimension to coleslaw. For a savory slaw, combine dressing with shredded napa cabbage, sliced radishes and green onions, and cilantro. For a sweet slaw, use shredded red or green cabbage (or some of each), sliced celery, and diced apple.

> 1 cup mayonnaise or 1/2 cup *each* mayonnaise and plain yogurt
> 2 tablespoons rice vinegar
> 1 tablespoon sugar
> 1 tablespoon soy sauce
> 1/2 teaspoon ground ginger
> 1/2 teaspoon sesame oil

In a bowl, whisk ingredients together until smooth. Use at once or cover and refrigerate up to 3 days.

Makes 1 1/4 cups dressing

The Creamy Soy Dressing at right also makes a good dip for raw vegetables. To get the thick texture necessary for dipping, use only mayonnaise for the base; the dip would be too thin with yogurt.

For dippers, select asparagus spears, snow peas, broccoli and cauliflower florets, Belgian endive, carrots, cherry tomatoes, or other garden-fresh vegetables.

German Potato Salad

A wonderful accompaniment to grilled chicken, grilled sausages, and cold cuts, this salad is easily transportable, making it a favorite for summer picnics and fall football games. It's best when served warm. If made ahead and refrigerated, reheat the salad in a microwave oven just long enough to take off the chill.

2 pounds thin-skinned potatoes

2 stalks celery, thinly sliced

1 small red onion, thinly sliced and rings separated

1/3 cup chopped parsley

4 teaspoons *each* all-purpose flour and sugar

1 teaspoon *each* dry mustard and celery seed

1/4 teaspoon salt

1/8 teaspoon cracked black pepper

1 tablespoon vegetable oil

1/3 pound sliced Canadian bacon, cut into matchstick-size strips

2/3 cup chicken broth

1/3 cup rice vinegar

In a pan, boil unpeeled potatoes, covered, in 2 inches of water until tender when pierced, 20 to 30 minutes. Drain and let cool. Peel potatoes and slice into a large bowl. Add celery, onion, and parsley. In a small bowl, combine flour, sugar, dry mustard, celery seed, salt, and pepper.

Heat oil in a 2-quart pan over medium heat. Cook Canadian bacon until lightly browned. Lift out and add to potatoes. Stir flour mixture into pan drippings. Add broth and vinegar. Cook, stirring constantly, until dressing boils and thickens slightly. Pour over salad and stir gently to coat. Serve while still warm. If made ahead, cover and refrigerate; let come to room temperature before serving.

Makes 6 servings

To keep vinegar in salad dressing from overpowering the flavor of wine, try mild rice vinegar or balsamic vinegar. Or you can take a tip from winemakers and add a little Zinfandel to vinaigrette dressing to make the flavors more compatible.

BLT Sourdough Salad Bowl

You could toss this full-meal salad in a bowl with croutons. But when presentation is important, we suggest serving it in a bread bowl. After the salad is transferred to plates, cut the bread into pieces and pour a glass of Zinfandel.

1   9-inch round loaf unsliced
     sourdough bread (1¹/₂ pounds)
¹/₂ cup homemade or purchased
     Italian-style salad dressing
2   tablespoons Zinfandel
¹/₄ cup grated Parmesan cheese
5   cups coarsely chopped lettuce
     (iceberg, romaine, or other)
1¹/₂ cups cherry tomatoes, cut in half
6   slices bacon, crisply cooked and
     crumbled
¹/₂ small red onion, thinly sliced
1   small avocado

Slice off a 7-inch circle from top of loaf. Cut out bread from center of loaf, leaving a ¹/₂-inch-thick shell. Cut removed bread into ¹/₂-inch cubes to make 2 cups and place in a shallow baking pan. Save remaining bread and the top for other uses.

In a bowl, whisk together salad dressing and wine. Sprinkle 2 tablespoons dressing and 1 tablespoon cheese over croutons; stir to coat all sides. Bake in a preheated 325° oven until golden brown and crisp, 20 to 25 minutes; cool.

Brush ¹/₄ cup dressing inside bread bowl. In a large bowl, combine lettuces, tomatoes, bacon, onion, and croutons. Peel and pit avocado; cut into ¹/₂-inch pieces and add to salad. Add remaining dressing; toss to mix. Place salad in bread bowl and serve.

Makes 2 full-meal servings

Some say sourdough was created by a miner who mixed a batch of dough and let it sit while he was away from camp. He returned to discover a bubbling mixture that smelled sour but made the best hot cakes he'd ever eaten.

Sourdough became a staple for prospectors from California to the Yukon and Alaska. They saved a little dough from every batch to provide the leavening for the next. Everywhere the fermented milk and flour starter traveled it acquired a different flavor from natural yeasts and bacteria in the air.

Chinese Chicken Salad

The recipe for this popular Asian dish calls for cooked chicken. You can make it from Roast Chicken with Honey-Hoisin Glaze (page 49), from roast chicken purchased at the deli, or by poaching chicken breasts. To take it along on a picnic, pack components in plastic bags and toss together at the site.

Plum Sauce Dressing:
- 1/4 cup bottled Chinese plum sauce
- 2 tablespoons vegetable oil
- 1 1/2 tablespoons rice vinegar
- 1 tablespoon orange juice
- 2 teaspoons sesame oil
- 1 teaspoon dry mustard
- 1 teaspoon grated fresh ginger

- 1 package (3 ounces) ramen-type noodle soup
- 2 cups shredded cooked chicken
- 1 carrot, shredded
- 1/4 pound bean sprouts
- 4 cups shredded iceberg lettuce (1 small head)
- 3 green onions and tops, thinly sliced
- 1/2 cup cilantro, coarsely chopped
- 1/4 cup slivered almonds, toasted
- 2 tablespoons sesame seeds, toasted

Prepare dressing: In a bowl, whisk together dressing ingredients until blended. Crumble soup noodles into a small bowl (discard seasoning packet); stir half of dressing into noodles. Let stand for 30 minutes.

Place chicken, carrot, bean sprouts, lettuce, green onions, cilantro, almonds, and sesame seeds in a large bowl; cover and chill until ready to serve. (If taking on a picnic, pack each item separately in a plastic bag and chill.) To serve, pour over noodles and remaining dressing and toss.

Makes 4 to 6 servings

Toasting heightens the flavor of nuts and seeds. For directions on toasting almonds, see page 13.

It's easiest to toast sesame seeds on top of the stove. Place them in an ungreased frying pan and shake the pan over medium heat for 2 to 3 minutes until seeds turn golden and begin to pop. Let them cool on a plate or paper towel.

Shaking Beef Salad

This Vietnamese full-meal salad is full of surprises: hot bites of juicy beef contrast with crisp cold greens; fruity olive oil smooths the bold garlicky flavor. Serve with French bread and wine for a leisurely weekend lunch or light supper.

- 1 tablespoon minced shallot
- 1 tablespoon minced garlic
- 1 tablespoon Thai fish sauce
- 1/2 teaspoon sugar
- 1/4 teaspoon salt
- 1/8 teaspoon pepper
- 1 pound boneless beef sirloin or top round, fat trimmed, cut into 1/2-inch cubes
- 1 tablespoon vegetable oil

Salad:
- 2 tablespoons *each* olive oil and rice vinegar
- 1/4 teaspoon *each* sugar and salt
- 1/8 teaspoon pepper
- 1 small red onion, thinly sliced and rings separated
- 1 head butter lettuce, washed and crisped
- 1 bunch watercress, washed and crisped

In a medium bowl, combine half of shallot, half of garlic, fish sauce, sugar, salt, and pepper. Add beef and stir to coat. Let stand for 30 minutes. Reserve vegetable oil to cook beef.

In a large bowl, combine olive oil, vinegar, sugar, salt, and pepper. Stir in onion; let stand 30 minutes. Just before serving, tear lettuce and watercress into bite-size pieces. Place in salad bowl and toss with onion dressing.

Heat reserved vegetable oil in a wok or wide frying pan over high heat. Add remaining shallot and garlic and cook for 10 seconds. Add beef and stir-fry until seared on outside and slightly pink in center, 1 to 1 1/2 minutes. Add to salad and toss.

Makes 4 servings

Chinese and Japanese cooks use soy sauce as an all-purpose seasoning. In Southeast Asia, salty, amber-colored, fish sauce is the seasoning of choice.

Don't be put off by the pungent aroma of the fermented fish extract; it dissipates upon cooking. Store fish sauce in a cool, dry place for up to one year.

Bean & Roasted Pepper Salad

A colorful alternative to traditional three bean salad, this delicious dish can be made with canned beans as a convenience for quick family meals. For a crowd, we prefer to cook beans from scratch (directions at right).

1 pound red bell peppers, roasted and
   peeled (page 21)
1 can (15 ounces) black beans
1 can (15 ounces) white kidney or
   cannellini beans
$\frac{1}{2}$ small red onion, thinly sliced
3 tablespoons olive oil
1 tablespoon white wine vinegar
2 cloves garlic, minced
$\frac{1}{2}$ teaspoon ground cumin
$\frac{1}{4}$ teaspoon *each* salt and pepper
2 tablespoons *each* chopped parsley
   and cilantro

Cut peppers into 1-inch pieces and place in a large bowl. Drain beans in a colander, rinse with cold water, and drain again. Add to peppers along with onion.

In a small bowl, whisk together oil, vinegar, garlic, cumin, salt, and pepper. Pour over bean mixture. Add parsley and cilantro; mix well. Cover and refrigerate for 1 hour for flavors to blend.

Makes 4 to 6 servings

You can create menu-planning magic with cooked beans on hand.

To cook beans from scratch, place 1 pound dried beans in a kettle with 6 to 8 cups water; boil 2 minutes, and let stand, covered, 1 hour. Drain. Add 6 cups water, bring to a boil, and simmer 1 1/2 to 2 hours.

Add salt to taste and additional seasonings after beans are tender.

One pound makes 4 cups of cooked beans.

Though the taco salad recipe at right calls for canned ripe olives, you may prefer to explore the varieties stocked by your local delicatessen.

Look for olives with a mild buttery taste, not too salty or bitter. And don't forget to remove the pits before tossing olives into the salad.

Taco Salad Supreme

A favorite with family and friends, this spicy, full-meal salad could be called "tacos in a bowl." Canned beans and olives and packaged taco seasoning and tortilla chips make it quick to fix. Serve warm with French bread and—of course—a young, fruity Zinfandel.

1 pound lean ground beef
1 medium onion, chopped
1 package (1$^1\!/_4$ ounces) taco seasoning
$^1\!/_4$ teaspoon pepper
1 can (15 ounces) red kidney beans, drained
1 can (2$^1\!/_4$ ounces) sliced ripe olives
$^2\!/_3$ cup shredded Cheddar cheese
1 small head butter lettuce, washed and crisped
1 large avocado
2 small tomatoes, diced
1$^1\!/_2$ cups taco-flavored tortilla chips, broken into pieces
Sour cream (optional)
Salsa (optional)

Crumble meat into a wide frying pan over medium-high heat. Add onion and cook, stirring often, until meat is browned and onion is soft, about 10 minutes. Pour off fat.

Stir in taco seasoning and pepper; mix well. Add drained beans, olives, and $^1\!/_4$ cup of the cheese; heat until cheese melts. Remove from the heat, cover, and keep warm.

In a salad bowl, gently tear lettuce into bite-size pieces. Peel, pit, and dice avocado; add to lettuce with tomatoes, tortilla chips, and the remaining cheese. Pour meat mixture into the bowl and toss. Garnish with sour cream and salsa, if desired.

Makes 4 to 6 servings

Italian Stuffed Artichokes

Since these artichokes are served at room temperature, they make a great buffet offering and picnic item as well as an elegant first course for a sit-down dinner. Rather than holding the artichoke leaf upside down, as you would when dipping in mayonnaise, pull the leaf between your teeth with the stuffing side up.

> 4 medium artichokes, 3 to 3¹/₂ inches in diameter
> 2 tablespoons vinegar
> ¹/₂ cup Italian-style dried bread crumbs
> ¹/₂ cup pesto (page 87) or purchased pesto

Prepare 1 artichoke at a time. With a knife, cut off stem and top third of leaves. Cut off thorny tips of remaining leaves with scissors. Drop into acidulated water (right) until ready to cook, then drain.

Place artichokes, bottom side down, in a pan with 2 inches of water and 2 tablespoons vinegar. Cover and simmer 15 minutes. Drain; let cool. Pull back leaves from center of each artichoke, pull out core of thistlelike leaves, and scrape out hairy choke with a spoon.

Mix bread crumbs with pesto. Stuff about 1 tablespoon of crumbs in center of each artichoke; press another tablespoon of crumbs between leaves.

Preheat oven to 350°. Stand artichokes in a deep baking pan; pour 1 inch of boiling water into pan around artichokes. Cover and bake 45 minutes or until artichokes are tender when pierced. (Poke a skewer through center down into heart to test.) Remove from water. Serve at room temperature.

Makes 4 servings

Artichokes are easy to cook, but they require special care to prevent discoloration. Use a stainless steel knife to trim artichokes, then drop them into acidulated water (2 tablespoons vinegar or lemon juice per quart of water) until ready to cook. The initial cooking directions at left prevent artichokes from turning dark and make it easier to remove the fuzzy chokes.

Caramelized Onions

When slowly cooked until their natural sugar caramelizes, onions make a marvelous accompaniment to hamburgers and grilled meats and poultry, and a terrific topping for pizza (page 70). The difference between the red and yellow onion recipes is the choice of seasoning.

   1 tablespoon *each* olive oil and butter
   3 large yellow or red onions, sliced
      1/4-inch-thick and layers separated

Red Onion Seasoning:
   1/4 cup Zinfandel
   1/4 teaspoon *each* dried thyme and salt
   1/8 teaspoon pepper

Yellow Onion Seasoning:
   2 teaspoons balsamic vinegar
   1/4 teaspoon salt
   1/8 teaspoon pepper

Heat oil with butter in a deep frying pan over medium heat. Add red or yellow onions, cover, and cook 5 minutes. Uncover and cook, stirring occasionally at first and more frequently as slices begin to wilt, until onions are very soft and caramelized, 30 to 40 minutes.

For red onions, add wine, thyme, salt, and pepper. Cook over medium-high heat until pan juices are reduced to a glaze, about 10 minutes.

For yellow onions, add vinegar, salt, and pepper. Cook until pan juices are reduced to a glaze, about 5 minutes.

Serve hot or at room temperature. Refrigerate up to 4 days and reheat before serving.

Makes about 1 1/2 cups (4 servings or enough to cover a 12-inch pizza)

Potatoes with Pesto

When fresh basil is plentiful, you can make several batches of pesto and freeze for future use. If you're short of time, purchased pesto tastes almost as good in this savory vegetable dish.

Pesto:
- 2 cups fresh basil leaves, washed and dried
- 2 cloves garlic
- ²/₃ cup grated Parmesan cheese
- ¹/₂ cup olive oil
- ¹/₄ cup pine nuts, toasted

- 2 pounds red thin-skinned potatoes, 1¹/₂ to 2-inch diameter
- 2 tablespoons olive oil
- Salt and pepper

Prepare pesto: Place basil, garlic, cheese, oil, and nuts in a food processor. Process until basil is finely chopped. Use pesto at once or place in small jars, adding a thin layer of olive oil to each jar to keep pesto from darkening. Refrigerate up to a week, or freeze for longer storage. Makes about 1¹/₂ cups.

Scrub unpeeled potatoes and cut into quarters or eighths, depending on size of potato. Place in a 9 by 13-inch baking pan. Add 2 tablespoons olive oil; sprinkle with salt and pepper. Bake, uncovered, in a 400° oven, stirring once or twice, until potatoes are tender when pierced, 40 to 50 minutes.

Add 3 tablespoons pesto to pan; stir to coat potatoes evenly. Return to oven for 2 to 3 minutes to heat through.

Makes 6 to 8 servings

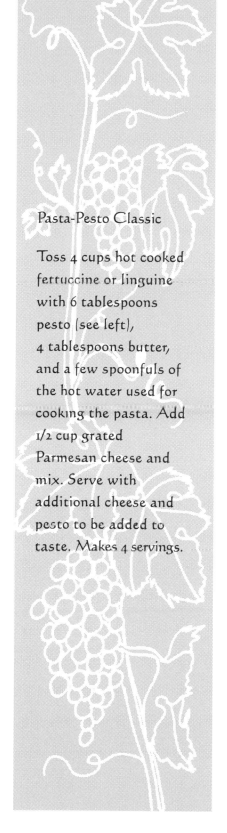

Pasta-Pesto Classic

Toss 4 cups hot cooked fettuccine or linguine with 6 tablespoons pesto (see left), 4 tablespoons butter, and a few spoonfuls of the hot water used for cooking the pasta. Add 1/2 cup grated Parmesan cheese and mix. Serve with additional cheese and pesto to be added to taste. Makes 4 servings.

Crusty Potato Pie

No need to fry individual pancakes; just pop this easy-to-make potato pie in the oven. It's an ideal side dish for buffets or becomes a meatless entrée when teamed with salad and bread.

3 large russet potatoes (1½ pounds)
2 large eggs
1 cup milk
¼ cup finely chopped onion
½ cup (2 ounces) shredded Gruyère cheese
2 tablespoons butter, melted and cooled
½ teaspoon salt
¼ teaspoon pepper
⅛ teaspoon ground nutmeg
Paprika

Preheat oven to 350°. Peel potatoes; shred to make 4 cups. As potatoes are shredded, place in a bowl of water to prevent discoloration.

In a large bowl, whisk together eggs and milk. Stir in onion, cheese, butter, salt, pepper, and nutmeg. Drain potatoes; squeeze to extract all moisture. Stir into milk mixture.

Pour into a greased 9-inch pie pan. Sprinkle paprika over the top. Bake for 45 minutes or until potatoes are tender and edges are crusty and browned.

Makes 6 servings

Tomatoes Provençal

A summertime recipe from sunny southern France focuses on the flavor of vine-ripened tomatoes.

  3   large tomatoes (about 8 ounces each)
      Salt and pepper
1/4 cup oil-cured olives
  2   cloves garlic, minced
  2   tablespoons chopped flat-leaf parsley
  2   tablespoons chopped fresh basil leaves
  2   ounces goat cheese (chèvre),
      crumbled, or 1 tablespoon grated
      Parmesan cheese
  1   tablespoon olive oil

Core and halve tomatoes; squeeze gently to remove seeds and juice. Place tomatoes, cut side up, in a small baking dish; sprinkle with salt and pepper.

Cut flesh off olive pits and coarsely chop. Combine with garlic, parsley, and basil. Spread mixture over tomatoes. Sprinkle cheese over the tops. Drizzle 1/2 teaspoon oil over each half.

Bake, uncovered, in a preheated 375° oven for 20 minutes or until tomatoes are soft.

Makes 6 servings

If you grow your own herbs, it's easy to snip off exactly what you need. Buying herbs at the market may yield more than you need at one time. To extend their storage life, wash in cold water, drain, and spin dry in a salad spinner. (Keep cilantro sprigs whole; pluck leaves from basil, and discard stems and blossoms.)

Place herbs in plastic bags, expel air, seal, and refrigerate. Reseal bags each time you open them; herbs will stay fresh 4 or 5 days.

Oven–roasted Ratatouille

You don't have to travel to France to eat good ratatouille. This oven-baked version is a snap to make and calls for less oil than those cooked on top of the stove. Baking in an open pan allows water inside the vegetables to evaporate and their natural sugars to caramelize.

Ratatouille tastes as good the second or third day as it does the first. Reheat in a microwave oven or serve at room temperature.

We take ratatouille along on picnics as a side dish for grilled chicken or as a dip for chilled artichokes in place of mayonnaise. Or try it as an omelet filling. Use 1 cup ratatouille, heated briefly in a microwave oven, for a 2-egg omelet.

- 2 tablespoons olive oil
- 3 large cloves garlic, minced
- 1/2 teaspoon *each* salt and pepper
- 1 medium eggplant, unpeeled and cut into 1-inch pieces
- 1 large onion, cut into 1-inch pieces with layers separated
- 1 large red bell pepper, seeded and cut into 1-inch squares
- 1 pound green or yellow zucchini, cut into 1/4-inch slices
- 1 pound Roma tomatoes, cored and cut into wedges
- 1/4 cup (lightly packed) fresh basil leaves
- 1 tablespoon balsamic vinegar

Mix oil, garlic, salt, and pepper in a large shallow roasting pan. Add eggplant, onion, bell pepper, and zucchini; mix well. Bake, uncovered, in a 400° oven for 30 minutes.

Add tomatoes; stir to turn all vegetables. Return to oven and bake for 20 minutes or until vegetables are tender. Stir once or twice near the end of baking time.

Shred basil. Remove ratatouille from oven; add basil and balsamic vinegar. Stir with a spatula to let vinegar absorb browned bits in bottom of pan. Serve hot or at room temperature.

Makes 8 servings

Balkan Vegetable Ragout

Some of the best vegetable ragouts come from European kitchens. Seasonings reflect national preferences and ingredients vary according to a home garden's bounty. This version gets a burst of flavor from paprika and black pepper.

- 3 tablespoons olive oil
- 1 large onion, cut into 1-inch pieces
- 2 cloves garlic, minced
- 1 tablespoon paprika
- 1 teaspoon dried thyme
- $1/2$ teaspoon pepper
- 1 can ($14^1/2$ ounces) diced tomatoes, undrained
- $1/2$ eggplant, unpeeled, cut into 1-inch cubes
- $1^1/2$ cups cauliflower florets
- 2 carrots, cut into $1/2$-inch rounds
- $1/4$ pound green beans, cut into 2-inch lengths
- 1 red bell pepper, seeded and cut into 1-inch squares
- 2 medium thin-skinned potatoes, cut into 1-inch pieces
- 1 cup canned beef broth
- 2 bay leaves
- $1/2$ cup frozen peas, thawed
- 1 teaspoon salt

Heat oil in a 6 to 8-quart pan over medium heat. Add onion; cover and cook, stirring once or twice, for 5 minutes. Add garlic, paprika, thyme, and pepper; cook 1 minute.

Add tomatoes, eggplant, cauliflower, carrots, green beans, bell pepper, potatoes, broth, and bay leaves; mix well. Bring to a boil; reduce heat, cover, and simmer, stirring occasionally, for 30 minutes. Scatter peas over the top. Cover and simmer 10 minutes or until vegetables are tender. Discard bay leaves; add salt.

Increase heat to medium high. Cook, uncovered, for 10 minutes or until pan juices are syrupy and reduced to about $1/3$ cup. Serve hot or at room temperature.

Makes 8 servings

You can add, subtract, or vary the vegetables in a ragout according to your taste. If you don't like cauliflower, use zucchini; if you're wild about potatoes, add another one.

Because vegetables lose their shape with continual stirring, use a bulb baster to scoop up juices for basting. If you use a spoon to baste, tip the pan slightly and scoop out as much liquid as you can reach without bruising the vegetables.

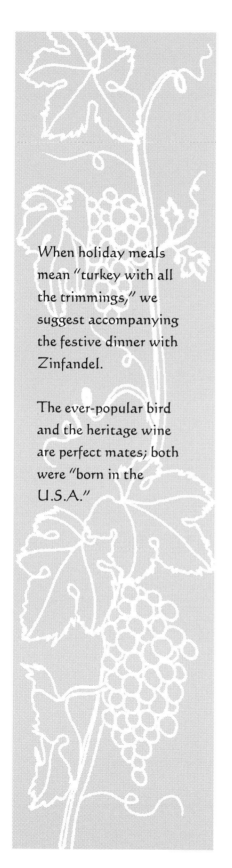

When holiday meals mean "turkey with all the trimmings," we suggest accompanying the festive dinner with Zinfandel.

The ever-popular bird and the heritage wine are perfect mates; both were "born in the U.S.A."

Calabaza

Sweet, creamy butternut squash and corn give this colorful Mexican side dish its natural sweetness. It makes a fine accompaniment to grilled meats, roast poultry, and wild game, or you might try it as a replacement for the traditional candied yams at Thanksgiving.

2 tablespoons vegetable oil
1 butternut squash (about 2 pounds), peeled, seeded, and cut into $3/4$-inch cubes
1 medium onion, coarsely chopped
1 clove garlic, minced
1 can (14$1/2$ ounces) diced tomatoes, undrained
1 red bell pepper, seeded and cut into 1-inch squares
1 package (12 ounces) frozen cut corn
$1/2$ teaspoon *each* salt and dried oregano
$1/4$ teaspoon pepper

Heat oil in a 5-quart pan over medium heat. Add squash, onion, and garlic; cover and cook, stirring once or twice, for 5 minutes.

Add tomatoes and bell pepper. Cover; reduce heat and simmer 15 minutes. Add corn, salt, oregano, and pepper. Cover and simmer 5 minutes or until squash is tender. Increase heat to high, uncover, and cook until most of the liquid has evaporated, 3 to 4 minutes.

Makes 8 servings

Desserts & Drinks

Gilded corkscrew
19th century

If you think wine and dessert don't mix, you're in for a surprise. From Berry Sorbet and Biscotti to Bittersweet Chocolate Cake, all of these mouth-watering "final touches" are created to complement wines like Late Harvest Zinfandel.

Some, such as Steamed Persimmon Pudding and the accompanying Whipped Hard Sauce, include wine as an ingredient in their recipes.

Also tucked into this chapter are simple directions for making icy punches for summer parties or a flavor-filled hot drink for holiday entertaining.

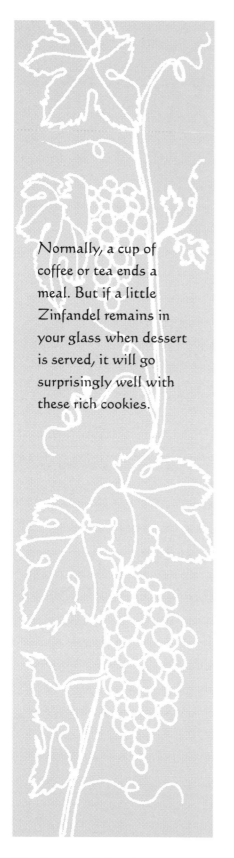

Normally, a cup of coffee or tea ends a meal. But if a little Zinfandel remains in your glass when dessert is served, it will go surprisingly well with these rich cookies.

Chocolate Almond Bars

Whether your family prefers creamy milk chocolate or dark semisweet, these nut-studded treats will bring smiles to their faces. Stored in an airtight container, they last for days—or until discovered.

1 cup butter
1 cup packed brown sugar
2 egg yolks
1 teaspoon vanilla extract
$1/4$ teaspoon salt
$1 1/4$ cups all-purpose flour
$1/2$ cup rolled oats
8 ounces milk or semisweet chocolate, coarsely chopped
1 cup sliced almonds

Preheat oven to 350°. Grease a 9 by 13-inch baking pan.

In the large bowl of an electric mixer, beat butter and brown sugar until fluffy. Beat in egg yolks, vanilla, and salt. Add flour and rolled oats; mix well. Pat dough in an even layer in prepared pan.

Bake 15 to 20 minutes or until lightly browned on the edges and a wooden pick inserted in the center comes out clean.

Remove pan from oven and turn off heat. Sprinkle chocolate over cookies. Return pan to oven for 2 to 3 minutes or until chocolate is soft. With a spatula, spread chocolate over the top; sprinkle with nuts.

Cool on a wire rack, then cut into bars.

Makes 4 dozen cookies

Biscotti

These crunchy, twice-baked cookies are Italian classics. They're served to dunk in wine or strong espresso coffee.

3 cups all-purpose flour
3 teaspoons baking powder
$1/2$ teaspoon salt
$1/2$ cup butter, softened
1 cup sugar
3 large eggs
1 teaspoon anise extract
2 teaspoons grated orange peel
1 teaspoon grated lemon peel
1 cup whole unblanched almonds

Preheat oven to 350°. Grease 2 baking sheets.

Sift flour, baking powder, and salt into a medium bowl. In the large bowl of an electric mixer, beat butter and sugar until fluffy. Beat in eggs, one at a time. Then beat in anise, orange peel, and lemon peel. Add flour mixture; mix well. Stir in almonds with a heavy wooden spoon.

Divide dough into 4 equal portions. On a floured board, shape each portion into a rope about 10 inches long. Place on greased baking sheet and press into a band about $1^1/2$ inches wide. Repeat with remaining dough, spacing bands at least 2 inches apart.

Bake 25 to 30 minutes or until firm. Cool 5 minutes. With a heavy chef's knife, cut diagonal slices about $3/4$-inch-thick. Lay slices flat on baking sheets and return to a 300° oven 15 to 20 minutes or until toasted. Let cool, then store in an airtight container.

Makes about 4 dozen cookies

Instead of Port and English walnuts, try this almond-laced Biscotti with Late Harvest Zinfandel, California's entry as an after-dinner drink.

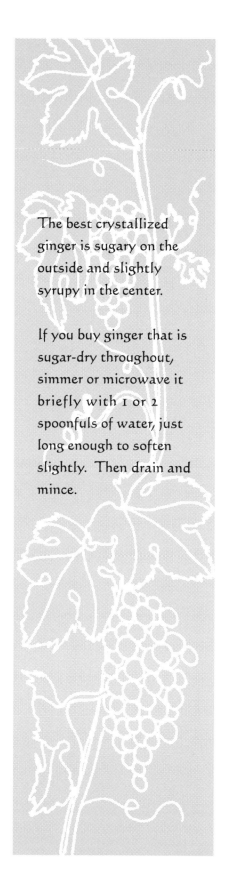

Ginger Snaps

Crisp on the edges and chewy in the middle, this cookie is simply addictive. It gains its intense flavor from the addition of both ground and crystallized ginger.

2 cups all-purpose flour
2 teaspoons baking soda
2 teaspoons ground ginger
1 teaspoon ground cinnamon
$1/4$ teaspoon salt
$2/3$ cup butter, softened
1 cup sugar
1 large egg
$1/4$ cup molasses
$1/4$ cup minced crystallized ginger
$1/2$ cup sugar for coating

Preheat oven to 350°. Sift flour, baking soda, ground ginger, cinnamon, and salt into a medium bowl.

In the large bowl of an electric mixer, beat butter and 1 cup sugar until fluffy. Beat in egg and molasses. Add flour mixture and crystallized ginger; mix well.

Roll dough into balls about 1 inch in diameter and place them 2 to 3 inches apart on an ungreased baking sheet. Place $1/2$ cup sugar in a small bowl. Moisten the base of a flat-bottom glass with water, then dip the glass in sugar, and press the glass on a ball of dough to flatten it slightly and coat with sugar. Repeat this procedure to flatten and sugar-dust each cookie.

Bake 10 minutes or until cookies are set on the edges but slightly soft in the centers. Let cool on wire racks, then store in an airtight container.

Makes 3 dozen cookies

Dried Fruit Strudel

Here's a lucious bake-and-serve dessert to keep on hand for company dinners or quick family meals. Once you wrap the tangy–sweet dried fruit and nut filling in filo, simply freeze the unbaked rolls.

- 1 package (8 ounces) mixed dried fruit (pitted prunes, pears, apples, apricots, and peaches), coarsely chopped
- 1/2 cup *each* dried cherries and raisins
- 2 cups water
- 1/2 cup sugar
- 1/2 teaspoon ground cinnamon
- 1/4 teaspoon ground allspice
- 2 tablespoons Late Harvest Zinfandel
- 1/4 cup finely chopped pistachios
- 6 sheets filo
- 1/3 cup melted butter for brushing filo
- Powdered sugar

Combine all dried fruits, water, sugar, cinnamon, and allspice in a 3–quart pan. Cook over medium heat until sugar is dissolved. Reduce heat, cover, and simmer 45 minutes or until fruit is tender and liquid has been absorbed. Stir near end of cooking. Stir in wine and nuts; let mixture cool.

Lay a sheet of filo horizontally on work surface and brush with butter. Cover with a second sheet and brush with butter. Spread 1 cup of filling in a strip 2 inches from the bottom edge. Fold bottom edge over filling and roll up jelly–roll style. Cut in half to make 2 strudels and place, seam side down, on an ungreased baking sheet. Brush with butter. Repeat with remaining filo and filling.

Cover and refrigerate strudels if you plan to bake within 24 hours, or freeze.

To bake, preheat oven to 375°. Bake strudels 20 minutes (25 to 30 minutes if frozen) or until golden brown. Let cool 30 minutes before cutting. Dust with powdered sugar.

Makes 12 servings

It's said that wines produced in areas where food is grown taste good with those foods.

From California's orchards come a bounty of plums, pears, peaches, apples, apricots, cherries, and pistachios. Vineyards yield Thompson Seedless raisin grapes as well as Zinfandel wine grapes.

Packing red wine in the picnic basket eliminates the need for ice and, best of all, a Zinfandel tastes great with a variety of foods—from appetizers to the Plum Tart end of a meal.

Faux Plum Tart

Beautiful to behold, the classic French tart is fussy to make, fragile when cut, and best eaten within a few hours after baking. For easy-going cooking and casual dining, we prefer this rustic tart made with a buttery cakelike base that complements the fruit topping.

1 cup all-purpose flour
$^1/_2$ teaspoon baking powder
$^1/_4$ teaspoon salt
$^1/_2$ cup butter, softened
$^1/_2$ cup sugar
3 large eggs, separated
2 tablespoons orange juice
1 teaspoon vanilla extract
1 pound black or red plums (or both), halved, pitted, and sliced $^1/_2$-inch-thick
2 tablespoons sugar mixed with $^1/_4$ teaspoon ground cinnamon
$^1/_4$ cup currant jelly

Preheat oven to 350°. Grease a 12-inch pizza pan. In a small bowl, combine flour, baking powder, and salt. In a large bowl, beat butter and sugar until fluffy. Beat in egg yolks, one at a time. Beat in orange juice and vanilla. Add flour mixture; mix well.

In another bowl, beat egg whites until they hold firm peaks. Fold $^1/_3$ of egg whites into batter to lighten, then fold in remaining egg whites. Spread batter in prepared pan. Overlapping slices slightly, place plums on batter, starting at the outer edge and working toward the center. Sprinkle with cinnamon-sugar mixture.

Bake 30 to 35 minutes or until plums are tender and edges of cake are lightly browned. In a small pan, heat jelly over low heat until liquid but not bubbly. Brush a thick layer of jelly over plums. Let tart cool before serving.

Makes 10 to 12 servings

Fruit Cake Bon Bons

For a sweet ending to tree-trimming parties and yuletide buffets, serve these tiny cakes on a silver or glass tray adorned with toyon or holly leaves. Best of all, they need no aging.

> 1 can (6 ounces) frozen orange juice concentrate, thawed
> 1/2 cup molasses
> 1 box (15 ounces) raisins
> 1 pound diced mixed glacéed fruit
> 1 1/4 cups all-purpose flour
> 1/2 teaspoon ground nutmeg
> 1/4 teaspoon *each* ground allspice and ground cinnamon
> 1/8 teaspoon baking soda
> 1/2 cup butter, softened
> 2/3 cup sugar
> 3 large eggs
> 1/2 cup chopped pecans or hazelnuts

Preheat oven to 350°. Combine orange juice concentrate, molasses, and raisins in a 3-quart non-reactive pan. Bring to a boil; reduce heat and simmer, uncovered, for 5 minutes. Remove from heat and stir in glacéed fruit. Let cool. In a bowl, combine flour, nutmeg, allspice, cinnamon, and baking soda.

In the large bowl of an electric mixer, beat butter and sugar until fluffy. Beat in eggs, one at a time. Add flour mixture; mix well. Stir in raisin mixture and nuts.

Line mini-muffin pans with small baking cup liners. Place about 1 tablespoon batter in each liner. Bake for 18 minutes or until a wooden pick inserted in center comes out clean. Let cool on wire racks, then store in an airtight container up to 1 week. Freeze for longer storage.

Makes about 6 dozen

Taking along a bottle of wine as a gift for the party host or hostess is always a nice gesture. There's no need for fancy wrap; just tie a ribbon around the neck and sign the label with your name, date, and greeting.

Expect your host to save the wine for another festive occasion.

If you're the wine recipient, tell the donors that you'll drink a toast to them when you open the bottle.

Bittersweet Chocolate Cake

Chocoholics agree that this is the ultimate dessert. Adding pumpkin purée makes the cake very moist. You can serve it in two ways: as an impressive four-tiered, triple-chocolate treat with cream filling and glaze (see directions below), or simply by cutting the layers into wedges and topping with chocolate cream filling.

1¼ cups all-purpose flour
⅓ cup unsweetened cocoa
1½ teaspoons baking powder
1 teaspoon baking soda
½ teaspoon *each* salt and ground
    cinnamon
3 large eggs
¾ cup *each* granulated sugar and
    packed brown sugar
1½ cups canned pumpkin
1 teaspoon vanilla extract
1 cup vegetable oil
4 ounces bittersweet chocolate,
    finely chopped

Chocolate Cream Filling:
3 tablespoons sugar
2 tablespoons unsweetened cocoa
1 teaspoon vanilla extract
1 cup whipping cream

Glaze:
¾ cup powdered sugar
½ cup unsweetened cocoa
⅓ cup whipping cream
4 tablespoons butter, cut into chunks

Preheat oven to 350°. Lightly grease and flour 2 cake pans (8-inch rounds).

"Chocolate and Zinfandel are complementary because both have intense flavors and high aromatics. These aromatics we usually attribute to fruity (orange, berry, strawberry, raspberry, etc.) and to floral (rose, gardenia, etc.) smells. In addition, chocolate has roasty toasty 'base' aromatics that enhance, and are enhanced by, the wetness of wine along with the sweet-sharp (acid), full-body qualities in Zinfandel.

Choose a complex Zinfandel to match chocolate."

—Edy Young,
    San Francisco-based
    chocolatier and
    Zinfandel lover

Sift flour, cocoa, baking powder, baking soda, salt, and cinnamon into a medium bowl. In the large bowl of an electric mixer, beat eggs with granulated sugar and brown sugar until creamy. Add pumpkin, vanilla, and oil; mix well. Add flour mixture and mix well. Stir in chocolate.

Spoon batter into prepared pans. Bake 30 to 35 minutes or until a bamboo skewer inserted in centers comes out clean. Transfer pans to racks and let cool 15 minutes. Turn cakes out of pans onto racks and let cool completely.

Prepare chocolate cream filling: In the large bowl of an electric mixer, combine sugar and cocoa. Stir in vanilla. Add cream and beat until cream holds soft peaks.

Prepare glaze: Sift powdered sugar and cocoa into a small heavy pan. Stir in cream. Place over low heat and stir until smooth. Add butter, a chunk at a time, and stir until glaze is smooth and slightly thickened. Remove from heat and let cool until thick enough to pour over cake.

Assemble cake: Slice each cake layer in half horizontally to make 4 thin layers. Place 1 layer on cake plate. Spread $1/3$ of cream filling over the top. Repeat with 2 more layers, covering each with $1/3$ of filling. Place final layer on top. Drizzle glaze over cake; some will run down the sides. Refrigerate until time to serve.

Makes 10 servings

Steamed Persimmon Pudding

Soon after vintners complete their crush, the pointy Hachiya persimmon ripens—a signal for holiday baking. This dark, moist, spicy steamed pudding can be made ahead and refrigerated, or frozen for later use.

1 cup all-purpose flour
1 teaspoon ground cinnamon
$^1/_4$ teaspoon *each* ground allspice and salt
$^1/_2$ cup butter, softened
1 cup sugar
2 large eggs
1 teaspoon *each* lemon juice and warm water
2 teaspoons baking soda
1 cup persimmon purée
2 tablespoons Late Harvest Zinfandel
1 cup *each* raisins and chopped pecans
Whipped Hard Sauce (recipe at left)

Grease 4 pound-size cans (those used for vegetables) or 2 pound-size coffee cans.

Combine flour, cinnamon, allspice, and salt in a medium bowl. In the large bowl of an electric mixer, beat butter and sugar until fluffy. Beat in eggs, one at a time. In a small bowl, combine lemon juice, water, and baking soda; stir into persimmon purée. Add flour mixture to creamed mixture alternately with purée. Stir in wine, raisins, and nuts.

Spoon batter into prepared cans, filling cans no more than $^2/_3$ full. Cover each can tightly with foil. Place cans on rack in steamer over boiling water. Cover and steam until a bamboo skewer inserted in center of pudding comes out clean, $1^1/_4$ to $1^1/_2$ hours.

Let cool 10 minutes, then turn pudding out of cans and cut in 1-inch thick slices. If made ahead, cool, cover, and refrigerate. To reheat, wrap slices in foil and steam until hot. Serve pudding warm with hard sauce.

Makes 8 servings

Perfect over persimmon pudding, mincemeat pie, or other holiday desserts, this Whipped Hard Sauce gets its zing from Zin.

In a bowl, blend together 4 tablespoons softened butter, 1 cup powdered sugar, and 1 tablespoon Late Harvest Zinfandel.

Whip 1/4 cup whipping cream until it holds soft peaks; fold into the creamed mixture.

Cover and chill up to 12 hours.

Pears Poached in Spiced Zin

Simmering pears in a tangy wine sauce transforms them into a simple but elegant ending to any meal.

> 2 cups Zinfandel
> ¹/₂ cup sugar
> 6 black peppercorns
> 6 whole allspice
> 2 whole cloves
> 1 cinnamon stick
> 1 bay leaf
> 4 medium-firm ripe Bartlett or
>   Bosc pears

Combine wine, sugar, peppercorns, allspice, cloves, cinnamon stick, and bay leaf in a non-reactive pan. Bring to a simmer over medium heat.

Peel pears with a vegetable peeler, keeping stems intact. As you peel each pear, place it in the liquid. Simmer, uncovered, until pears are barely tender, 10 to 15 minutes. Turn pears occasionally in the syrup to cook evenly.

Lift out pears with a slotted spoon and place in a wide bowl. Increase heat and simmer syrup until reduced by one-half. Pour syrup over pears and let cool.

Refrigerate, covered, for 24 hours.

To serve, place pears in dessert bowls. Strain syrup over the fruit.

Makes 4 servings

This recipe for Red Wine Sauce comes from "Poetry in Cookery" cookbook, published in 1897. (Zinfandel was often called "Claret" in those days.)

"One bottle of Claret, 6 ounces of sugar, 2 ounces of large raisins, same quantity of blanched almonds cut in long, thin pieces, cinnamon, rind of 1 lemon. Mix all together and boil 1 minute. Remove the lemon rind and cinnamon stick and serve."

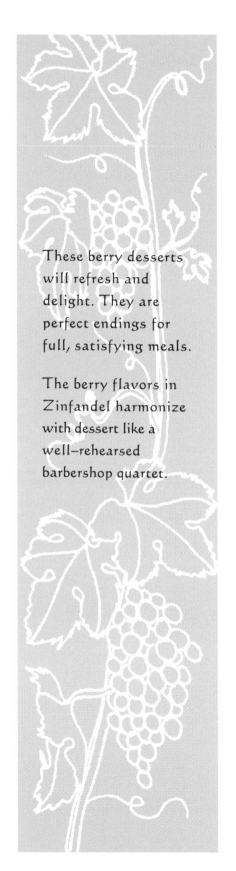

These berry desserts will refresh and delight. They are perfect endings for full, satisfying meals.

The berry flavors in Zinfandel harmonize with dessert like a well-rehearsed barbershop quartet.

Berry Sorbet

A combination of fresh seasonal berries and fruit juices, this sorbet is served both as a frosty finish or as a palate refresher between courses.

> 3/4 cup water
> 1/2 cup sugar
> 2   cups unsweetened blackberries, boysenberries, or raspberries, or some of each
> 2   tablespoons orange juice
> 1   tablespoon lemon juice

Heat water and sugar in a small saucepan until sugar dissolves; let cool. Purée berries in a food processor; strain through a fine sieve to remove seeds. Combine sugar syrup, berry purée, orange juice, and lemon juice. Pour into a 9-inch square pan.

Freeze 3 hours or until firm. With a table knife, cut mixture into small pieces; whirl in a food processor until slushy. Spoon sorbet into a 1-quart container. Cover and freeze until firm, about 2 hours, or up to 1 week.

Makes 4 servings (3 cups)

Berry Brûlée

Sweet juicy berries, silky sour cream, and brown sugar broiled until it crackles—these are ingredients for a spectacular summer dessert that always gains attention.

> 1   cup small strawberries, hulled
> 1/2 cup *each* raspberries and blueberries
> 1/2 cup sour cream
> 2   tablespoons milk
> 1/3 cup packed brown sugar

Place berries in a shallow, oven-proof serving dish. Just before serving, whisk together sour cream and milk; pour over berries. Sprinkle brown sugar evenly over the top. Broil 4 inches from heat until brown sugar melts, 2 to 3 minutes. Once sugar begins to melt, it caramelizes quickly, so watch carefully to prevent burning. Serve immediately.

Makes 4 servings

Citrus Cooler

This effervescent and colorful punch makes an excellent choice for all festive occasions.

- 1 magnum (1.5 liter) White Zinfandel
- 1 bottle (33.8 ounces) sodium-free sparkling water
- 1 can (12 ounces) frozen tangerine juice
- 1 cup ice cubes or 1 block of ice
- 1 orange, thinly sliced
- 1 lime, thinly sliced

Chill wine and sparkling water.

In a 5-quart punch bowl, mix tangerine juice and wine. Add ice and sparkling water. Float orange and lime slices on top.

Makes 18 to 20 servings

Fragrant Punch

From pool parties to holidays, this aromatic wine punch turns all occasions into special events. In summer, ladle into glasses and garnish with a fresh blackberry or raspberry; in autumn, add a thin slice of orange.

- 2 cups boiling water
- 1 cinnamon stick
- 12 whole cloves
- 1 lime thin skin (zest), cut into strips
- 1/2 cup raspberry or blackberry jelly
- 1 bottle (750 ml) Zinfandel
- Ice cubes

In a non-reactive container, pour boiling water over a mixture of cinnamon, cloves, lime zest, and jelly. Let stand until water reaches room temperature; pour through a fine sieve. Combine punch base with wine and refrigerate up to 1 week. Serve over ice.

Makes 10 to 12 servings

These lighthearted drinks reflect the carefree times of summer holidays and celebrations.

Crisp and refreshing, the punches contain only one-half the alcoholic content of wine.

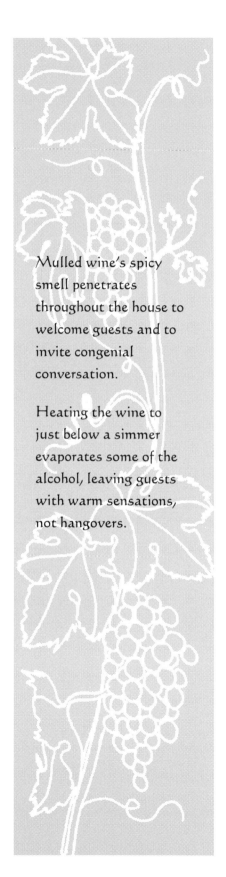

Mulled wine's spicy smell penetrates throughout the house to welcome guests and to invite congenial conversation.

Heating the wine to just below a simmer evaporates some of the alcohol, leaving guests with warm sensations, not hangovers.

Zin 'n Tea

When combined with ginger ale, this duo produces a refreshing cold drink for a hot summer day.

> 2 cups boiling water
> 2 tea bags
> 2 cups Zinfandel
> 1/2 lemon, unpeeled
> 1 tablespoon brown sugar
> Ice cubes
> Ginger ale

Prepare concentrate for the punch in a teapot or glass measuring cup. Pour 2 cups boiling water over tea bags; let steep for at least 10 minutes. Remove tea bags. Add wine, lemon, and brown sugar; stir to dissolve sugar. Refrigerate until ready to use.

To serve, first remove lemon from concentrate. Place ice cubes in a glass and fill with 1/2 concentrate, 1/2 ginger ale. Stir lightly to mix.

Makes 1 quart concentrate

Party–Time Mulled Zinfandel

Because Zinfandel has a berry flavor that gives this drink a natural sweetness, you may not need to add extra sugar. Apple juice may be added to the mixture, if desired.

> 1 tablespoon whole cloves
> 3 small oranges
> 2 cinnamon sticks
> 2 magnums (1.5 liter each) Zinfandel
> Sugar to taste

Poke cloves into the oranges, making sure the surface of each orange is evenly covered.

Place oranges in a 6-quart non-reactive pot; add cinnamon sticks, wine, and suger. Warm on low heat, gradually adjusting heat as needed, so the mixture is kept just under a simmer. Ladle into glasses and serve warm. You can leave the mulled wine on low heat for the duration of the party.

Makes 24 servings

Party Planning

The recipes in this book were developed especially to go with red Zinfandel wine. In our testing, we included wine styles from light and fruity to concentrated and bold. Young and older vintages from Zinfandel-growing regions throughout California were also compared.

Our findings? All of the Zinfandels tested received high marks although individual taste preferences differed. However, any party featuring a good bottle of Zin and these recipes will be successful.

Dinner Parties

At formal dinners, a different Zin may be served with each course, starting with a light style and progressing to more intense flavors. A small glass of Late Harvest Zinfandel might accompany dessert.

For BBQs, potlucks, and casual entertaining, you may wish to pour the same vintage throughout the meal.

Fill wine glasses only 1/2 full to allow room to swirl the wine and release the fragrance. Set a separate glass for each style served and allow one pour per wine plus a little extra.

Party Tips

Invite guests to arrive no more than an hour before you plan to serve dinner. Pour either a White Zinfandel or a young, light, slightly chilled red Zinfandel and pass one or two appetizers.

When guests are invited to be seated for dinner, we make sure that they know whether they should leave their wine glasses or bring them to the table.

One bottle (750 ml) of Zinfandel equals 24 ounces or six pours. One pour (4 ounces) fills a standard stemmed wine glass 1/2 to 2/3 full. Plan to serve three pours per person at wine receptions, two pours with pre-dinner appetizers.

Zinfandel and Late Harvest Zinfandel should be served at room temperature, 68 to 74°F; White Zinfandel should be chilled.

To open a wine bottle, cut the capsule (seal) 1/2-inch down from the top of the bottle and remove the upper part to expose the cork. Leave the rest of the capsule on the bottle; it's part of the design.

Remove the cork when you're ready to use the wine. Wine "breathes" in the glass, not the bottle. If you're opening an older Zinfandel (over 20 years), remove the cork just before you plan to drink it; older wines are fragile and tend to lose their bouquet shortly after being poured.

Selecting & Cellaring Wine

Touring wineries is certainly the most romantic way to buy wine. You have a chance to see the vineyards and learn a little about the winemaking process.

Once you select your wine, where will you store it? Whether you plan a cellar for your wine library or make space for a few bottles, we offer some storage tips.

Buying Wine

There are two ways to buy wine —direct from the winery or from a wine merchant at a local shop, supermarket, or discount store. Each option has advantages.

On a trip through California's wine-producing regions, you'll have a chance to sample different vintages and styles of Zinfandel in winery tasting rooms. Though you pay retail prices for wine, buying it here assures correct storage prior to the sale.

If you encounter hot weather on your wine tour, don't leave bottles in your car. Wines warmed above 90°F tend to degrade. If you buy wine by the case, ask the winery to ship it to you.

Though you may not be able to taste the Zinfandel you buy at a wine shop, you will usually get expert help in finding a Zin to match your meal and budget. You may also uncover some great bargains through close-outs or special sales.

Supermarkets and discount stores may have the lowest prices but no assurance of professional assistance. Our suggestion: buy a bottle and take it home to try; if you like it, buy a case. Remember, great bargains sell quickly.

Storing Wine

From wine cellar to closet—no matter where you stash your bottles, here are a few guidelines.

Wine should be stored in a cool, dark, quiet place at a constant temperature (50-60°F) to keep it from aging too rapidly and losing its finesse. Sunlight and florescent bulbs also affect flavors.

Keep wine away from motors that produce vibrations. Bottles need to be secured if you live in an area prone to natural disasters.

Wine can be stored in its original case. Just be sure that the wine in the bottle is in contact with the cork. A controlled humidity of 58% keeps corks from drying out.

For maximum quality, let wine rest at least a week before opening.

Index

(Continued on page 110

....Continued from page 109)

RESOURCE GUIDE—WINE-FRIENDLY FOOD SERIES

Publishing wine-friendly food cookbooks involves delightful research and surprising discoveries. Home-kitchen testing each recipe, then savoring several Zinfandel wines with each dish, is an experience I wish I could share with you. Unfortunately, I am not able to invite you into my kitchen or to join me on winery visitations. But this is an exciting time to learn about wine and food.

To keep information current, I am using several techniques to let you, the reader, share in my discoveries. These communication methods range from the Toyon Hill Press web site, to e-mail messages and TOYON e-CLIPS, my e-mail newsletter, to the reliable postal service.

You can visit my Toyon Hill Press web site at **www.toyonhillpress.com.** Current information is posted. I have developed a list of the wineries producing Zinfandel and how to get wines sent to you (if you live in a 'reciprocal state' to which the wineries can ship). I present my discoveries of new and unusual recipe ingredients, cooking methods, and personal opinions about wine-friendly foods. I catalog sources for unique food products, spices, and cooking tools that you can order shipped to your door. Also I give suggestions for substituting ingredients to use in the recipes for speed and ease of preparation as well as hard-to-find components. There are recipes, unique to the web site, as well. Through the web site, graphic information, like pictures and maps, is available to you. Links to many other wine, cooking, winery, and travel sites are presented for your investigation. Join me at **www.toyonhillpress.com** for some delightful discoveries.

Your opinions, thoughts, and innovative suggestions are important to me. Comments from you will help me plan future publications. Your comments may appear on the web pages or in my e-mail newsletter, TOYON e-CLIPS, unless you tell me otherwise.

To share your joys, comments, and queries about Zinfandel and its many delights contact me by e-mail at **margaretsmith@toyonhillpress.com** or write me a letter at **Toyon Hill Press, 118 Hillside Drive, Woodside, CA 94062-3521.**

Margaret A. Smith, Publisher

Toyon Hill Press

Wine-Friendly Food Series Cookbooks

Rhône Appétit, Food to Serve with American Rhône Varietals
by Jane O'Riordan. An experienced chef, Rhône wine producer, and daily home-maker presents her recipes for Rhône wine-friendly foods.

Companions At Table, Food to Serve with American-grown Italian Varietals
by Barbara J. Braasch and Margaret Acton Smith. Recipes from wine lovers to match with Sangiovese, Barbera, Moscato, Pinot Grigio, Arneis, and more.

Zinfandel Cookbook, Food To Go With California's Heritage Wine
by Janeth Johnson Nix and Margaret Acton Smith. Over 100 home-kitchen tested recipes from Appetizers to Desserts to serve with Zinfandel wine.

☎ Toll-free telephone orders: **1-800-600-9086**
Have your MasterCard or VISA ready.

⌨ E-mail orders: **margaretsmith@toyonhillpress.com**

💻 Visit our website at **www.toyonhillpress.com**.

✉ Postal orders: **Toyon Hill Press, 118 Hillside Drive, Woodside, CA 94062-3521, USA**

🗐 Fax orders: **1-650-851-5579**

☽ Office Telephone: **1-650-851-9086**

I wish to order the following books:

_____ **Rhône Appétit**   Paperback, $17.95

_____ **Companions At Table**   Paperback, $17.95

_____ **Zinfandel Cookbook**   Paperback, $17.95

California residents please add $1.49 sales tax per book.   Shipping: $4.00

_____ Check Enclosed

_____ MasterCard or _____ VISA Card   Number _____

Name on card: _____Exp.date: month_____ year_____

Ship to name: _____

Address:_____

City: _____State: _____ Zip: _____

Telephone (____) _____

FREE: _Toyon Clippings_ newsletter |___| Place my name on your mailing list.

CALL TOLL-FREE AND ORDER NOW

I understand that I may return any books for a full refund,
for any reason, no questions asked.